THE SECOND VOYAGE OF *SWAN*

PORTLAND _____ 45°N

UNITED STATES

BEAUFORT, N.C.

SAN DIEGO

——— 30°N

SAN CARLOS   GULF OF
                  MEXICO
MEXICO

OKEECHOBEE
WATERWAY

CUBA

PAZ

ORRO

CAYMAN IS.

1990   ACAPULCO

TRADE WINDS

——— 15°N

CURRENT

GULF OF
TEHUANTEPEC

PERLAS
ISLANDS

SWAN

The
Second
Voyage

SWAN

The Second Voyage

JIM MOORE

SHERIDAN HOUSE

First published 1994
by Sheridan House Inc.
145 Palisade Street
Dobbs Ferry, NY 10522

Library of Congress Cataloging-in Publication Data

Moore, Jim, 1936–
    Swan : the second voyage / Jim Moore.
        p.   cm
    ISBN 0-924486-45-7 : $22.95
    1. Swan (Sailboat)   2. Voyages and travels.   I. Title.
G440.S95M67   1994
910.4'1—dc20   93-45463
                                                            CIP

Drawings and photos by the author

Design by Jeremiah B. Lighter

Printed in the United States of America

ISBN 0–924486-45-7

As we have so little say in the selection of our parents, I feel fortunate indeed to have been raised by loving parents whose common sense, traditional values, and wonderful sense of humor made their children's lives a joy.

To my mother and to the memory of my father, I dedicate this book.

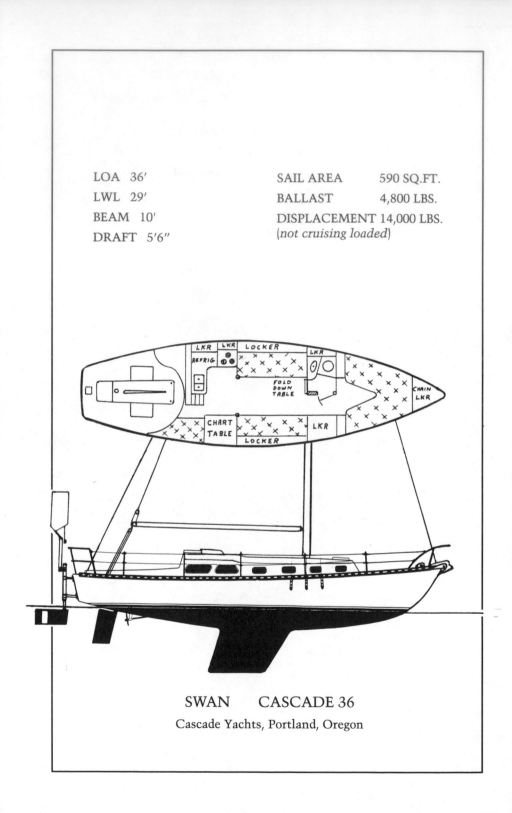

LOA 36'

LWL 29'

BEAM 10'

DRAFT 5'6"

SAIL AREA   590 SQ.FT.

BALLAST   4,800 LBS.

DISPLACEMENT 14,000 LBS.
(not cruising loaded)

LKR LKR LOCKER   LKR

REFRIG

FOLD
DOWN
TABLE

CHAIN
LKR

CHART
TABLE   LKR

LOCKER

SWAN   CASCADE 36

Cascade Yachts, Portland, Oregon

Preface

AT A GATHERING of cruising sailors in a waterfront bar, I stood listening to a raucous group of weather-beaten seadogs who were reliving their past voyages, complete with colorful embellishments. I eased away before it was my turn to regale them with yet another "harrowing" sea story.

I sat down at the far end of the bar next to a charming young couple whom I had met earlier in the marina where our boat was moored. They had been severely bitten by the cruising bug and had South Pacific stars in their eyes.

These would-be cruisers were aware that my wife Molly and I had sailed the seas on the other side of the world. They had read my first book, *By Way of the Wind*, the story of our four-year circumnavigation aboard our 36-foot sloop, *Swan*, and they were brimming over with questions about the pristine outer islands of Fiji, the coral labyrinth of Australia's Great Barrier Reef—and was doubling the Cape of Good Hope really scary?

Their contagious enthusiasm and unbridled optimism took me on a nostalgic flight back through the years to the mid-1970s when Molly and I were fledgling sailors caught up in a similar state of excitement about our cruising plans.

As we talked, their questions shifted from the exotic aspects of long-distance voyaging to the day-to-day routines and the unique problems one encounters living the cruising life; plain and simple questions like the ones Molly and I had asked or wondered about years before.

I suddenly realized that this receptive couple was hanging on my every word. The young woman was taking notes on a napkin. It wasn't just another inconsequential conversation at a bar. My advice would most likely have a strong influence on their approach to cruising. I also realized that I, like those hidebound, yarn-spinning sailors across the room, had strong opinions about blue-water yachts and what the cruising life was all about. My thoughts and priorities on the subject had evolved over a long period of trial and error, and had, for the most part, been set in stone. However, resisting the urge to preach the cruising gospel according to Jim Moore, I carefully prefaced my advice with the same words I often use in letters responding to readers of *By Way of the Wind*, who write to ask for advice both specific and general: "This is what worked for us."

I would like that phrase to work as a caveat throughout this book, too. Since the days when we built *Swan*, and throughout our cruising experiences, we have shamelessly embraced the supposition that "good plagiarism is better than bad originality." *Swan* is a composite of the best features of numerous boats, as well as our own innovations. Similarly, our reluctance to spend time and effort reinventing the wheel has led us to incorporate good ideas and procedures for sailing and living aboard from many other cruisers. Yet each crew has different aims and needs, and sometimes a system or method that works well on one boat will be a failure on another.

This is the story of a two-year, 10,000-mile voyage from Hawaii to the east coast of the United States via the Panama Canal, with a sojourn in the Sea of Cortez. It is in some ways a sequel to our circumnavigation story, and it is also a "nuts-and-bolts" book, with specific tips on boatbuilding, sailing, and living aboard woven into the narrative—as painlessly as possible, I hope. After 50,000 blue-water miles, these are some of the things that work for us. I hope you'll find them useful, too.

So, please come aboard and join Molly and me as we embark on *Swan's* second voyage. You can have the quarter-berth.

You do like Mexican food, don't you?

LOOKING BACK, IT IS DIFFICULT to pinpoint exactly when the seed of the idea for a second voyage took root. The notion lurked beneath the surface even before the first one had ended.

In the beginning, our plan was to take a block of time out of our workaday lives to do something exciting and adventuresome, and we had done just that. The first voyage had lasted longer than we had anticipated and had far exceeded even the boldest of our dreams. The time had come to make some long overdue payments to the piper, who had grown extremely impatient, so we never seriously discussed the possibility of a second voyage. It was out of the question—at least for the time being.

Four years earlier, when we had sailed shakily into the sunset on our first voyage, we'd had only enough "freedom chips" to see us through a three- or four-year cruise, and we had played fast and loose with the long-term financial picture. We couldn't get away with that forever. Prudence dictated that any future cruising could not be done without giving due consideration to the realities of age—as much as we hated to admit it.

Swan did not fit the mold of a weekend sailer. She was purely a cruising boat, but we had no immediate plans to put her up for sale. We weren't ready for the cruising question to be settled with such absolute finality.

One morning while we were sipping coffee in the cockpit and going over the numbers in the anemic bank account, Molly settled the question of our immediate future with one remark: "Well, if we're going to starve to death, wouldn't it be a lot more fun doing it in Hawaii?" It took me about 10 seconds to agree tentatively, and within 30 seconds it was in stone. Living aboard and working in Hawaii was the closest thing that we could think of to actually cruising.

We had dallied in Portland, Oregon for six weeks doing slide presentations, attending back-to-back parties, and basking in the attention that our earth-girdling voyage had afforded us. It was September 1981. Winter was waiting in the wings. It was time to make our escape to Hawaii.

It was a typical gray misty morning on the Oregon coast when we sailed across the Columbia River Bar and ventured forth into the Pacific Ocean.

Time had not dulled our memories of the apprehension we had felt when we first crossed this dangerous bar as greenhorn sailors. I recalled thinking at the time that if we had to lose our boat, it would be better to do it on a reef in the South Pacific or some other exotic place than on a sandspit on the Oregon coast.

The apprehension we felt on the present passage was of another kind. Our concerns were not so much about the potential dangers involved with getting to our destination, they were about finding a niche for ourselves when we got there. Mooring facilities were at a premium in Honolulu, with long waiting lists for slips. And how, precisely, would we earn a living?

On the plus side we had friends there, and had spent enough time in the islands that we were not harboring any illusions about what lay ahead.

Ocean Passages for the World made this passage sound so simple: "Proceed south ard until within about 300 miles northwest of San Francisco and thence proceed to Honolulu."

A steady Force 4* nor'wester drove *Swan* south through the dark oily swells under jib and reefed main. We always undersailed the boat on the first day out after a long stay in port to acclimate ourselves to the motion of the boat. Our experience had shown us that it is easier to prevent seasickness than to cure it.

*See Beaufort Wind Scale

2

Four days into the passage we had the waypoint on the port beam and bore off smartly to the southwest, flying the reacher and storm trysail, logging 155 miles for the noon-to-noon run.

On the afternoon of the sixth day, in the vicinity of 36°N, 133°W, the wind began to falter. By nightfall there wasn't the slightest trace of a breeze—but there was plenty of slop! We spent a miserable night trying to get some rest while *Swan* rolled heavily in the running sea.

Thus began a 10-day siege of unrelenting nothing. We had sailed squarely into the North Pacific High; a windless cell of high pressure that migrates slowly with the seasons. The "thence proceed to Honolulu" all but ceased.

We had no idea how large an area the high-pressure cell covered, or what sector of it we had entered. If it reached as far south as 30°N, which was very possible, and we continued on our course of 235 True, we could be in it for 600 miles. *Swan's* motoring range was 440 miles, and the thought of enduring the noise and heat of motoring that far would have been unacceptable even if we'd had the range.

Our compromise plan was to sail as much as possible by taking advantage of any puffs of wind that came our way, and to motor a few hours each day to guarantee a certain amount of daily progress.

Being stuck in a belt of calms was not a new experience for us. Over the years we had developed a routine that enabled us to cope with them reasonably well. First in importance is to accept the fact that meaningful progress has essentially stopped— don't fight the problem. Fussing over the chart and fiddling with speed/time/distance tables is frustrating and akin to trying to detect movement of the hour hand on a clock. Second, make the situation as comfortable as possible, mentally and physically. Eliminate all unnecessary noise.

Regardless of how calm the ocean is, there is almost always a swell, which causes the sails to slat, chafing them and one's nerves as well. I can abide about five minutes of slatting sails.

We dropped the main and put the sailcover in place where

3

it stayed for more than a week. It is surprising how many conscientious sailors would never consider spending a day in an anchorage with the mainsail uncovered, but will run for days on end on a passage flying a spinnaker or headsail, with the furled main lying exposed unnecessarily to the tropical sun.

On about the third roll that collapsed the reacher, we took it down and put up the doldrums rig: the whisker pole set with the flat-cut working jib stretched tight as a banjo string. This arrangement could only be used when the wind was abeam or abaft the beam, because the whisker pole limited the sheeting in of the sail.

The rig was set in precise order. The jib was poled out and the sheet tightened until the sail was just taut. Small adjustments of the pole topping lift and the foreguy were made until the foot and leech tension were equal. When this was done, the jib sheet was winched in firmly with a cautious eye to the compression load on the whisker pole. The result was a drum-tight, dead-quiet, chafe-free panel or resistance to airflow.

In ghosting airs, Vane, our "trusty" windvane, steered an erratic course in the general direction of our destination, as if he had been nipping the compass alcohol. The whole affair was so horribly inefficient that it would have caused a racing sailor to fall sobbing on the deck in a state of abject despair. But it was peaceful, and we were moving.

We attempted to treat these potentially frustrating periods as if we were at anchor with a bloody long row to shore. Awnings were in place, ports and hatches were open, we read and worked on projects as we would have in an actual anchorage. The mate baked bread, cooked elaborate meals, and tried, usually unsuccessfully, to coax or coerce me into playing cards. However, I was sometimes enticed into playing if the stakes she proposed were more interesting than mere money, given the reasonably good odds that a neighbor or the kids wouldn't be dropping by unexpectedly.

I recall one of Molly's becalmed galley binges, somewhere in the South Atlantic in the third year of our first voyage, while lying dead in the water in the horse latitudes. Suddenly she announced triumphantly that she had, at long last, perfected her stove-top biscuit mix. It would be an enduring contribution to the body of culinary knowledge and galley expertise; her name would be listed in the acknowledgements of cruising cookbooks for years to come, and future generations of grateful galley slaves would refer to it reverently as "Molly's Mix." It wasn't until a year or so later, in Hawaii, that she discovered that she had reinvented Bisquick.

Each afternoon we motored for three or four hours, south by west, on the thin hope that by some quirk of fate, or divine intervention, the Northeast Trades might have edged north of 30° degrees north latitude, even though a weather anomaly such as that would be classified as a minor meteorological miracle.

At dusk we shut off the engine and *Swan* would coast slowly to a dead stop. The abrupt silence was oppressive. So much so that I was forced to mix gin and tonics for medicinal relief, and to use some of the ice that the freezer was producing so prolifically because of all the time spent motoring on this passage.

Whenever we did a lot of motoring we built up reserves of ice if there was room in the freezer. We made ice in two rectangular aluminum containers that were secured in a vertical position directly against the freezer cold plate. The tall, narrow design of the containers prevented water from slopping out, provided they were not filled to the brim, even when the boat was heeled over a fair amount. When the water froze, we put the containers in the sink to thaw, or melted them quickly under a stream of fresh or salt water, just enough to allow the ice to slide out.

The ice was stored in plastic bags or containers to serve as frozen ballast to replace the frozen foods as they were consumed, making the refrigeration system more efficient and building up a reserve of ice for those periods when little motoring was done.

When refilling the ice containers, we cooled the relatively warm fresh water from the tanks with a piece of ice, or filled them from a jug of cold water from the refrigerator to minimize the warming of the cold plate at the spot where the containers and the plate made contact. This allowed the cold plate to absorb heat more uniformly.

Near the end of a long period between provisionings, *Swan* became a floating ice wagon. Word about this would get out, which meant that our boat and her valuable cargo were always welcome in remote anchorages in the tropics—especially at Sundowner Time. We didn't miss many cruising parties.

For a brief period, five days into the calm, a breeze wafted in from the north. The glassy sea was suddenly covered with small wavelets, eliminating the relentless glare. *Swan* moved ahead, sparking hope in our hearts.

We were in the process of taking down the doldrums rig when the fickle breeze abruptly died again, leaving us with sporadic catspaw puffs and our touch-and-go one-knot pace.

The sea conditions and crisp horizon were a navigator's dream. On most days we established our position with a running fix of the sun. At about 1000 I observed the sun's altitude with the sextant, and when the sun crossed the meridian of longitude that we occupied (local apparent noon) I took the noon latitude. Molly or I would work out the sights and advance the 1000 line of position (LOP) along the course line for the distance run between sights (about two or three miles at our snail's pace) and cross it with the noon latitude, fixing our position.

On days that the moon was visible and at a proper angle in relation to the sun, I would take a sight of the moon and cross it with the noon latitude, giving us a fix in a matter of a few minutes.

This was the sum total-of our navigational efforts for the average day while we were ghosting through the calms, except for keeping a rough mental accounting of the way of the ship between fixes.

With the motoring, the ghosting, and the favorable current, we were averaging about 40 miles per day. Existing TransPac records were not in any great danger.

Trying to make a few miles at night was not worth the effort. After dinner we lowered the jib, twisted it into a loose roll, and lashed it to the lifeline, leaving the clew in the sailing position at the outer end of the whisker pole. The pole remained in place, secured by its topping lift, the foreguy, and the jib sheet.

Ever since the time I let the jib halyard jerk from my grasp during a passage in the South Pacific, which necessitated a frightening trip up the mast in rough seas, we never again unsnapped the halyard shackle from the sail cringle unless the headsail was being bagged. When a sail was lowered temporarily, as in this instance, we unfastened the top sail hank from the forestay and snapped it to a loop on the pulpit for that purpose, leaving the halyard *attached to the cringle* at all times. This eliminated the possibility of losing control of the halyard. The slack in the wire was then taken up on the halyard winch.

When it was necessary to fasten or unfasten the halyard, we held onto the wire, not the shackle, because it was less likely to jerk out of our hand should the boat roll sharply. A trip up the mast in rough seas provides one with a nice sea story, but it isn't worth it, I can assure you.

More than a week had elapsed since we had seen a ship. The San Diego-Honolulu great circle track was the only shipping route in the vicinity, and it was well south of our position. Visibility was excellent, so we had few qualms about turning on the anchor light and a bright cockpit light and sleeping for two-hour intervals during the night.

We normally arose at 0500 to resume our meander to the south, often motoring for an hour or so to start the day with the feeling that we were accomplishing something. Our psychological trick of treating our plodding situation as if we were at a remote anchorage was beginning to wear thin after a week on the painted ocean.

Near latitude 31°N we were greeted at sunrise by a southern horizon blackened by line squalls. At this point, any change whatsoever in the weather was welcome.

The squalls were not the dangerous, electrically charged thunderhead type, so we started the engine and motored directly toward one that was due south of us. As we drew near it, we saw a wide swath of small white horses moving rapidly toward us across the water; little white-crested wavelets being formed almost instantly on what just moments before had been a glassy surface. We managed to get the whisker pole down and the jib sheeted in before the squall hit—and it hit hard.

It was glorious! The cold rain came down in blinding sheets, chilling my BVD-clad body. *Swan* heeled sharply for a moment, righted, and shot off toward the south at a gallop. I set Vane on a close reach and went dripping below, where the mate was frantically closing the ports and hatches. We were laughing like fools. We knew it wouldn't last, but it didn't matter. It was such a relief just to be sailing.

As the blustery little storm center moved by, Vane followed its perimeter winds until we were sailing due west, and then it was over. But it was the harbinger of a radical change in the weather pattern.

Squalls continued to march over the horizon in a steady stream for all of that day. Vane was like a fickle debutante with too many suitors. He would wander off after any one of them that came near, but generally we maintained a southerly course.

We then set about collecting rainwater. Drinking water is so vital that I believe one should top off the tanks at every opportunity.

The sails had been washed free from salt during the first squall, and we prepared for the next big one that came along in the afternoon by emptying the water jugs into the freshwater tanks and lashing them and two five-gallon plastic buckets on the foredeck.

As the squall approached we were flying only the jib to minimize the action of the boat as much as possible, and Vane was set on a beam reach. The jib sheet was reeved through a block well forward of its normal position on the toerail, to produce a belly in the sail. The jib halyard was then lowered about four feet, and the loose foot of the sail was inside the lifelines with the center portion gathered into a plastic five-gallon bucket.

The squall was a real classic. Rain fell in torrents. *Swan* sailed along smoothly in the calm seas on a beam reach, and water cascaded down the sail and into the bucket, filling it in a matter of seconds. We exchanged buckets and filled the jerry jugs.

Collecting rainwater and filling the tanks should be totally separate operations at sea. I think it is a mistake to connect a water catchment device directly to a storage tank because of the risk of polluting the fresh water with salt water. We filled the tanks direct from a catchment awning at anchor, but not at sea.

When all of the containers were filled, we squirted shampoo on our hair and took one of the all-time great passage showers, pouring whole buckets of water over our heads. We maintained proper attire for this—safety harnesses over our birthday suits.

Swan was making about four or five knots. In the deluge we couldn't see the stern of the boat. These are the times that people are lost overboard. The task at hand, or the excitement and fun of the moment takes all of our attention, opening the door for a potential accident. In high winds and frightening seas during a storm, we're usually thinking more about our own survival than anything else, and it would be hard to pry us off the boat.

Three of our cruising comrades have been lost at sea as I write this. Of the three, one for certain and perhaps two were lost because they were not wearing safety harnesses. This sad fact is always in the back of our minds.

In addition to 15 gallons or so thrown around recklessly during our bath, our efforts netted 30 gallons of sweet water, topping off the small tank, and nearly filling the large one.

Molly was down below drying her hair and chirping about how squeaky clean it was. She had an especially rosy, appealing appearance from the effects of the chilly bath, and was still wearing only the harness, which added a certain something that one wouldn't think it should, and it caused me to start wondering if she was possibly in the mood for playing cards. She wasn't.

A fresh breeze built steadily from the south-southwest.

Not exactly the dizection that we would have liked. We complained, but not loudly—wind was wind.

Latitude 30°N had somehow become more significant than what it was in reality: an east/west line on a chart. It was like "door number three." Our whole world lay waiting behind it.

But whatever lay on the other side, it could wait a little longer. It wasn't worth going to windward, even in the existing mild sea conditions, when we could sail faster and more pleasantly due west on a close reach. *Swan* sailed through the night, flying the working jib and single-reefed main, making a respectable five knots.

On the 18th day of this lingering passage, *Swan* crossed 30°N into the promised land. We had sailed 1410 miles. In 1977 we had made the 2020 mile crossing from San Francisco to Hilo, Hawaii in the same amount of time.

To our great surprise we intercepted the fringe of the Northeast Trades after a day of motorsailing in fluky winds. We held our south-southwest course for a full day to get more into the heart of the trade belt before we resumed our direct course.

Swan romped through the warm, white-crested seas with the wind on the quarter, making six knots, fish lines streaming. She was doing what she knows so well: running the westing down.

I have never experienced anything that compares to the feeling of pure freedom and the exhilarating satisfaction of running day after day before a steady tradewind in a well-found sailing yacht. On dozens of moonlit nights I have stood literally for hours leaning on the dodger, watching the action of the sea and listening to the sound of the bow cutting through the waves, while the sails, grayish-white in the moonlight, silently drive the ship through the night.

The world ashore is changing at a speed that boggles the mind, but the private world of a sailing vessel at sea has remained essentially unchanged for millenniums. The sea is the great equalizer. Politics, money, and one's station in life mean nothing in a storm at sea. The integrity of the ship and the competence of the captain and crew are all that matters.

The same sun, moon, and stars are there as guideposts now as they have always been. The same natural forces that create the wind and sea conditions haven't changed. The same tradewind routes exist now as they did when the great four-masters ran down through the Roaring Forties in the China trade. It's all there waiting.

On more than one of these moonlit nights, in one of my romantic flights of fancy, *Swan* has become a forest of masts and spars; shrouds, ratlines, and rows of deadeyes, complete with the pungent smell of tarred marline, as she runs in heavy trades under a full press of canvas, bound for Valparaiso around the Horn.

A grand and free run through the trades will banish to the foggy recesses of one's mind the memories of any hardships that might have been endured during the preparation years. They are the price of admission.

For six days we ran toward the islands with only the poled-out reacher driving the boat, averaging 135 miles per day. The forward hatch and leeward ports were open, which allowed the cooling breeze to course through the boat. The main boom was relegated to the function of a very substantial awning support as the wind was abaft the beam, and life was very pleasant indeed.

On Day 24 of this outrageously long passage, navigation took a decidedly more active part in the daily routine. Morning and evening star sights were added to the normal daily sun fix. Our approach to Honolulu would be a fair distance off the well-lighted north shore of Molokai. It was a comparatively easy landfall.

A three-star fix with an LOP of Jupiter thrown in for good measure placed us 70 miles northeast of Diamond Head on the evening of the 26th day. In the small hours of the morning Molly raised the Kalaupapa navigation light on Molokai, and we set our course for the Molokai Channel.

Landfalls are always exhilarating, no matter how many of them one has made, but this one was almost a letdown. We weren't continuing on to the South Pacific. We had come to Hawaii to work; to join the masses who, Thoreau said, "lead lives of quiet desperation."

Well, after giving it some thought, I had the feeling that spending a few years in the islands, toeing the mark, wasn't going to be all that desperate.

2

A MODERATELY HEAVY SEA was running in the Molokai Channel when *Swan* sailed into the lee of Koko Head in company with four U.S. Navy ships that were steaming toward Pearl Harbor.

We rounded Diamond Head and sailed in close enough to shore to check out the hustle and bustle along Waikiki Beach. It was early morning, but the beach was already dotted with tourists waiting to be fried in the tropical sun.

Vane was still in charge of the steering duties. He had done an exemplary job on the passage, and his enormous ego demanded that he be allowed to steer during the promenade past Waikiki. What he didn't know was that he would spend the next seven years stored in various sheds and garages, and end up languishing in a wood-shop loft, covered with all manner of boatyard fallout, sawdust, and a sprinkling of rat droppings.

One of the inalienable laws of mooring Tahiti Style, or Med Style if you are the Continental type, is that when it is attempted, at least 15 knots of wind must be blowing, gusting to 25, and a minimum of 40 people must have nothing else to do but rivet their attention on the center ring, where they are certain that a spectacle is about to unfold.

Besides the fixed laws, there are an undetermined number of contingencies—none favorable—that must be dealt with during the mooring maneuver without a moment's hesitation; similar to shooting pop-up targets in combat infantry training.

All the fixed laws existed as we approached the only open mooring slot, a very narrow one, in front of the Hawaii Yacht

Club (there is a large dock there now, and transient boats no longer moor Tahiti Style).

The first contingency we encountered was a bleach bottle that was serving as an anchor buoy, tethered by a length of floating polypropylene line. It had no business being there, as the water in front of the club is a right-of-way area, and the bottle was defying all known laws of physics by drifting upwind and what appeared to be up-current. It was straining mightily to get into the path of our boat, and I had no doubt whatsoever that in the line of duty it would willingly sacrifice its life by wrapping itself to death around our propeller shaft.

The second contingency, though less threatening in the immediate sense, was the boat, or rather the person aboard it, at the other end of the anchor line to which the bleach bottle was attached. It was the boat on the downwind side of the narrow slot that I fervently wished we were safely in.

On its deck stood a man who could not possibly have displayed more misery and anguish at the horrid thought of a boat occupying the space next to him. He looked first at us, then at the coveted space, and then stared disbelievingly at us as if we were the manifestation of the apocalypse. He made no positive moves such as putting fenders over the side to protect his boat's gleaming topsides, although we had put fenders out as a precaution.

As we motored slowly toward the slip, Molly lowered the stern anchor and I held the boat upwind of the approach line—cool and calm. Then the bleach bottle made its move. I hesitated for a moment, a gust of wind hit—and we lost our chance. *Swan* slowly swung downwind through a 90 degree arc, tethered by the stern hook, until we lay stern to the wind, pointed back toward the ocean.

From the corner of my eye, I noticed with chagrin that some of the diners on the upper deck near the railing had turned their chairs around for a better view of our act.

The mate chose this moment to make the remark: "This isn't the only island group in the Pacific where we could settle."

There was no use faking it. No one would believe that we

had chosen this moment to display our unique method of swinging the compass. We regrouped.

On the second attempt, embarrassed and more than a little ticked off, I went for it. I made an end run around the bleach bottle, skimmed in next to the flashy boat, slammed it in reverse, boiling the water as Molly snubbed the anchor line, and we skidded to stop in the dead center of the slot.

"Throw me your bow line," said a voice that I recognized immediately. It was Verne Russell, a member and one of the perennial good guys at the Hawaii Yacht Club. Over the years, as Port Captain and in other capacities, he has greeted countless cruisers as they arrived in Hawaii from all points of the globe.

Perhaps Verne had missed our little performance, because he cleated off the lines without comment. But it occurred to me that he may have been saving his remarks until we got up to the bar, where there was an appreciative audience. We took the cowardly way out and slinked off to the showers instead.

Our intention was to spend two weeks enjoying the club's hospitality while we systematically planned our assault on Hawaii's business community. At the end of the two weeks we had done an outstanding job of enjoying ourselves, and we didn't have the foggiest notion of how we were going to earn a living.

With our time up at the club, we moved to Keehi (kay'-hee) Lagoon on the outskirts of Honolulu, where we were to live aboard for most of the succeeding seven years.

Keehi Lagoon, known as just "Keehi" by its residents, was the last bastion for the liveaboard cruising sailor on the island of Oahu, and generally speaking, all of Hawaii, unless he had served his time on the long waiting lists for a marina slip. Its chief attractions were that it was free if one lived in the anchorage, and it was close to the Honolulu metropolitan area.

Honolulu is a magnet for nearly every old salt roaming the sea within the Pacific Rim. When the cruising kitty is suffering terminal anemia, and the dyed-in-the-wool cruiser cannot abide the thought of returning to the mainland rat race, he gravitates to Honolulu, and in the natural order of things, to Keehi Lagoon. We fit this mold perfectly.

It was our good fortune that our arrival in the crowded anchorage was timed just as a boat's anchor was being raised in preparation to leave. The boat was sailing for the South Pacific, and the choice space that it had occupied was open.

We quickly pounced on the vacated spot, which was fairly close to shore. The distance from shore was no small consideration as we faced the prospect of rowing to-and-fro each day in the tradewinds that sweep across the lagoon.

We put down two anchors in roughly 14 feet of water with both rodes streamed from the bow, but in opposite directions. *Swan's* primary anchor, a 35-pound CQR, was set with 150 feet of 5/16" proof coil chain toward the prevailing northerly winds. A 22-pound Danforth anchor with 165 feet of line and chain rode was set toward the south, from where the blustery "Kona winds" sometimes blow at gale force in the winter months, if one can seriously refer to the rainy season in Hawaii as "winter."

The Kona anchor line was fastened to the primary anchor chain about two feet above the water by means of a large ring and shackle, with the remainder of the line secured to the bow cleat and coiled on deck.

When the wind was southerly, the resulting strain on the Kona rode was borne by the anchor chain, which eliminated the chafing problems involved with taking the line, under load, directly to the bow cleat.

A short length of heavy nylon line, sheathed in rubber hose for chafe protection, was fastened to the bow cleat, led over the twin bow roller, and shackled to the chain. About two feet of chain was then payed out at the anchor windlass, creating a small bight, or loop, placing the load on the bow cleat rather than the windlass. This also eliminated sound transmission through the chain as it moved over the bottom (See Fig. 1 and 1A).

Occasionally, because of fluky wind periods, the rodes would become intertwined. This problem was easily sorted out by unshackling the Kona anchor line.

When we wanted to take the boat out for a daysail, which wasn't very often, we left the dinghy tethered to the Kona anchor to "guard" our choice spot.

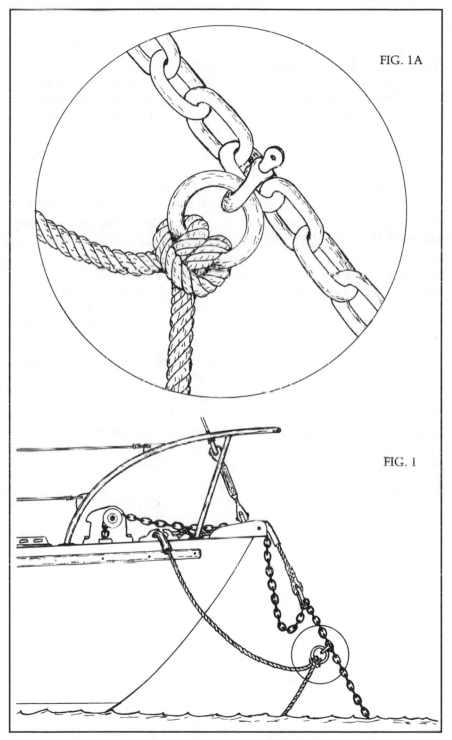

FIG. 1A

FIG. 1

FIG. 1   *Two anchor rodes streamed chafe-free from bow*
FIG. 1A   *Anchor rode shackled to chain*

As a result of this anchoring arrangement our swinging radius was small, even with the relatively large scope on each anchor, and *Swan* was secure for the long term, even in the worst of conditions. This would be proven unequivocally in less than a year when hurricane Iwa roared through the Kauai Channel, with its perimeter winds pummeling the boats in Keehi Lagoon.

Anchored near *Swan* was the 56-foot ketch *Starshine*, owned by Doug and Linda Balcomb, who, with their daughter Heather, had sailed extensively in the South Pacific. We had first met them in Hilo, Hawaii in 1977 when the two boats had arrived from the mainland a day apart—the first blue-water work for both boats. We saw them from time to time while sailing in the Hawaiian Islands, and later we spent some time together while cruising in New Zealand. We had become good friends.

The Balcombs had been in Honolulu long enough to have made a few superficial inroads into reestablishing themselves on the fringe of normalcy. Doug had a job, more or less, working on boats in the Ala Wai Boat Harbor, a state-run mooring facility near Waikiki. His "business vehicle" was an old two-toned station wagon, faded-green and iron oxidation (Hawaii is full of such two-tone vehicles). In the back of the wagon he carried a collapsible workbench and a box of tools, many of which had suffered the ravages of the sea.

When Doug told me that they had an actual address and a real mailbox, I thought we had lost them for sure.

Molly applied for work in her profession as a nurse at state and local government institutions and in the military. While she was waiting for the wheels of government to turn, she managed to land a job with a fruit-packing company, demonstrating fancy ways to slice pineapples in the lobbies of Waikiki hotels. Each day she rode the bus across town wearing a long flowing muumuu and carrying a ridiculously long knife in a scabbard.

At times she would return to the boat late in the evening. I was accustomed to seeing her in shorts, and when she came down the companionway ladder wearing that long dress, silhouetted in the subdued light with the knife in her hand, she could just as well have been Tony Perkins coming down the stairs at the Bates Motel. The sight was especially chilling if I happened to be taking a shower and opened the head door just as she came down the ladder.

One evening Doug rowed over to our boat and asked me if I had any varnishing experience. Having varnishing experience is normally a condition of life for a boatowner, at least among cruisers who rarely hire out their varnishing, or little else for that matter. But *Swan* was built within eyeshot of a 40-foot piece of floating furniture whose owner's right hand had practically evolved into a varnish brush during the 20 odd years that he had owned the boat. As a result of this sobering object lesson, *Swan* does not have a square inch of varnished wood on her, inside or out.

I answered no to Doug's question.

"Well you'd better learn quickly," he said. "I touted you as the best man with a varnish brush east of Taiwan. You start work tomorrow morning at eight o'clock."

This began an informal working alliance between Doug and me that grew into a partnership that would last seven years. It was one of the special relationships in my life.

Our basic natures could scarcely have been more different. I am, to a fault, an organized, orderly man, and Doug, well, isn't. We never made the fatal error of trying to convert each other, but just enough of our personal characteristics rubbed off between us to leaven the relationship. The most important ingredients of our partnership, the critical elements that made it fly, were a solid bond of trust and a disinclination to erode away our partnership, and friendship, by bickering and blaming each other when things went wrong—and they went wrong fairly often in the early years.

Our business day began on the lower deck of the Hawaii Yacht Club each morning where the coffee urn was steaming and a few of the regulars were gathered, Verne Russell being one of them.

Verne, at this juncture, failed to recognize two rising stars of commerce when he saw then. Our manner of dress no doubt influenced his less than favorable assessment of our future in the world of business.

We wore shorts and thongs, and usually some nondescript T-shirt. A favorite of Doug's had "Suck 'Em Up" emblazoned across the front of it.

One of our first big jobs was replacing the teak decks on a large powerboat that was built before the Great Depression. We needed a large quantity of teak to complete the job, which the owner had agreed to pay for up front. It was important that we get the best deal possible, and to do that it was necessary for us to pass ourselves off as legitimate businessmen—a tall order indeed.

I have a slight telephone phobia, and a discerning listener can sometimes detect it. It makes me sound like I'm not a legitimate businessman. Doug has an excellent presence on the telephone, and if I were a homeowner I would purchase siding from him over the phone in a heartbeat. So he handled the pricing of the teak on the telephone.

However, he wasn't prepared for a question put to him by an oriental lumber dealer. The fellow asked Doug for his company's name. Doug's phone presence suffered somewhat as he fumbled with the question for a moment, until he recalled one of Verne Russell's more pointed barbs. Verne had suggested that we name our company "Clown Shipwrights." This was the only name Doug could come up with off the top of his head, so he repeated it to the oriental fellow. "Ah so, Crown Shipwrights," the lumberman said, substituting an "R" for the impossible to pronounce "L" in the word "clown."

It was just too good. We filed papers with the state of Hawaii for incorporation as Crown Shipwrights.

The deck job had many problems to overcome, but we successfully completed it along with other work on the boat, and in the process, we established a small niche for our fledgling company in the boat-repair business.

At the same time that we were replacing the deck on the powerboat, we were refurbishing a 47-foot fiberglass ketch for a Honolulu businessman. The job started as small cosmetic work, and as is so often the way with boats, it grew into a major refit—chainplates, rigging, hardware, and dozens of smaller jobs.

The owner was entertaining thoughts about long distance cruising, but his needs and desires were such that a boat of the size he owned wasn't large enough.

We had become friends with the owner, and we would occasionally have cocktails on the boat before leaving on evenings when he was there.

During one of these respites, an 85-foot steel ketch out of New Zealand arrived in the Ala Wai. The boat had been built on speculation in a New Zealand yard and was enroute to Los Angeles to be placed on the market. It was about the size boat that our client had in mind.

On the following day, the owner, his wife, Doug, and I went aboard the 85-footer for a Cook's tour. For several reasons, it wasn't the right boat, but the seed was planted—and it germinated quickly.

Within a matter of a few weeks, the venerable firm of Crown Shipwrights was 100 percent involved with the interior design and modification of plans for a steel ketch to be built in New Zealand.

We set about the business of closing our newly opened shop, storing equipment and preparing to fly to Auckland, New Zealand, as owner's representatives, to oversee the construction of a 90-foot yacht.

In the middle of all of these exciting developments, the forces of nature chose to remind us how vulnerable we were.

A full weather watch had been in effect for a few days, monitoring a tropical storm that was developing a few hundred miles south of the Hawaiian Islands. For a time it was fairly stationary, then it began moving north, threatening the islands, and was subsequently upgraded to hurricane strength and officially named Iwa (Eva).

During the morning hours we listened to the hurricane update on the car radio. At noon, the reports stated that the hurricane would hit the island of Oahu or pass through the Kauai

Channel, which divides Oahu from Kauai, in the evening hours.

Doug had moved *Starshine* to a slip in the Ala Wai when an opening there had occurred. Their name had been on a waiting list for a slip for months, and it had finally reached the top of the roster. (Openings for larger boats occurred more frequently than for boats of *Swan*'s size in the Ala Wai Boat Harbor.)

As *Starshine* was secure, or at least stuck with her situation, Doug lent me a 35-pound Danforth anchor to use as a storm anchor. I loaded it into the massive trunk of a hulking 1973 Chevrolet that we had recently purchased. Like Doug's car, it sported the Hawaii two-tone—the other color being blue.

An hour or so past noon I picked up Molly at her current job, which was bugging people to buy things that they didn't need on the telephone. She hated that job, understandably, and I don't know how she stood it as long as she did.

When we arrived at Keehi, we were alarmed at the conditions that already existed in the lagoon. Perimeter winds of the advancing hurricane were blowing from the south-southeast and whipping up mean-looking white-capped waves, and it was raining hard. My interpretation of the hurricane progress reports had apparently been wrong. I hadn't anticipated the arrival of the first winds until evening.

A large trimaran had already dragged her anchor, and was a scant 100 feet or so to windward of *Swan*. I counted a total of 11 boats upwind of our boat. The majority of them were unattended, and some were secured to poorly maintained moorings or anchors. I doubted that their mooring lines were equipped with adequate chafe protection to withstand the trouncing that was surely in store for us. We viewed these boats as 11 potential headaches.

We loaded the anchor into the dinghy and rowed against the stiff wind along the docks where the water was slightly calmer, until we were about 250 yards diagonally upwind from *Swan*. From this vantage point we made a furious run at the boat with the beam wind setting us hard to the north, and made it to *Swan* without a moment to spare.

22

Getting the unwieldy anchor on board the heaving boat from the wildly bucking dinghy in a driving rain taxed all of my strength and patience, neither of which do I possess in any great amount.

I had intended to set the storm anchor using the dinghy; a plan that was completely out of the question in the prevailing conditions, so we did the only thing that was left: We heaved the anchor to windward from the bow.

The mate unearthed a 40-foot length of chain from the lazarette, which I shackled to the anchor. I then fastened 200 feet of one-half-inch nylon line to the chain, and together, on the heaving deck in the blinding wind and rain, we gave the anchor and the balled-up hunk of chain a mighty and uncoordinated heave over the pulpit. The 100-pound mass of flailing iron sailed through the air in a graceful arc, landing about two feet in front of the boat, and a loop of chain tore the starboard running light from its mounting in the process. The light hung there swinging by its wire, which prompted me to utter some lively and incisive comments.

I payed out 50 feet of slack line and cleated it off. The anchor was probably fouled and its value was questionable. But it was better than nothing out there if the Kona anchor dragged, or more probable, if a dragging boat fouled the rode.

Anchored about 600 yards north, and downwind from us, were our friends Carson and Katy Jefferson on their sailboat, *Via Mariah*. We arranged to meet them on a VHF talking channel at certain times and we monitored Channel 16 the remainder of the time. They were using substantially the same anchoring system as we used. A glut of boats were anchored in the space between *Swan* and *Via Mariah*.

We triple-tied our dinghy close astern of *Swan*, took down the awning, and dogged down all hatches and ports. Molly filled the thermos bottle with coffee and heated up some leftover spaghetti. There was nothing else we could do but listen to the radio reports and wait.

Rather than describe in narrative form the events of that memorable night, I have transcribed the notes that I scribbled on a pad of paper during the onslaught of hurricane Iwa on November 23, 1982. I have omitted a few esoteric entries that would only confuse the train of thought.

1810—Eye of hurricane Iwa passing near Kauai—winds ferocious here—I can't believe our anchor is holding.

1830—White water all over lagoon—wind gusting 70 knots—90 knots in channel—two boats dragged past, missed rode.

1910—Blue schooner anchored to windward parted Kona rode—swung toward us in breaking seas—girl on board alone doing all the wrong things—tourists getting rare show in Waikiki.

1930—Boat dragged over our CQR chain—he managed to get a hook down—*Swan* rolling heavily—no place to run—must fight it here—radio says Navy ships put to sea from Pearl Harbor—Navy battle group headed for Pearl diverted north—Hotel Street girls will have to wait another day.

1950—Honolulu blacked out—Keehi black as coal—one AM radio station operating—gloating disc jockey—jerk!

1955—VHF contact *Via Mariah*—Carson and Katy alive and well—boats dragging down on them—invited them to row up for cocktails—no contact *Starshine*.

2025—Kona rode like banjo string—boat insurance premium suddenly seems cheap—large sea running.

2050—Wind shifting to west—no let-up in force—boat very close to port—Kona anchor *very dear* to my heart—two boats sunk north end lagoon.

2055—Nearly had to crawl to foredeck to check gear—wind shrieking—set record for longest pee off stern in Keehi Lagoon history.

2130—Message from Carson—boat dragged down on French singlehanding girl—sheared off her bowsprit—dismasted an anchor—how demoralizing—fortunately she has *lots* and *lots* of friends.

2200—Marina docks breaking up—boat impaled on steel protrusion—bless Kona anchor's little galvanized heart.

2230—Wind definitely diminishing—may be out of the woods.

2330—Molly crashed and burned on settee—TV working on one channel—watching Johnny Carson's monologue—drinking whiskey and soda—good riddance to Iwa.

0100—Rinsed salt off my tired body—checked for chafe—winds manageable now—Honolulu still blacked out for most part.

0700—November 24, 1982—Anchorage completely changed— new neighbors—gave them "thumbs up" for our mutual survival—preponderance of boating community "dense packed" at leeward end of lagoon—we never dragged an inch that I can tell—I can't remember anything in years that concerned me as much as the Kona anchor—one boat to the south of us—10 dragged away or went away.

0830—Molly is baking a pie for our Thanksgiving potluck dinner with crews of: *Via Mariah, Starshine, Quantro,* and *Swan*— emphasis on "Thanks" this year.

FINDING A SAFE HAVEN for *Swan* while we were in New Zealand was our number-one priority, especially after what we had just been through. The Ala Wai Boat Harbor waiting list, which had our name on it, was still in the "years to go" stage for the size slip we required.

There was a marina at Keehi Lagoon, the one that was hit fairly hard during the hurricane, that had a shorter waiting list, but our name was not on it. After some heavy persuasion, the manager of the marina agreed to put *Swan* in a slip that was temporarily vacant. She would be moved as required until a permanent berth was available.

Carson and Katy on *Via Mariah* offered to keep an eye on *Swan* and attend to small maintenance jobs, such as keeping the batteries charged and rinsing her off occasionally while we were away. For this service we gave them our two-toned car.

Our New Zealand experience was broadening and financially rewarding. We spent over a year on the boatbuilding project, and made many friends in that country.

In 1978 we had visited New Zealand in *Swan*, and we met the people and saw the country as visitors, but you really get to know people of other countries when you're no longer regarded as purely a tourist. It is a fairly good indication that you have achieved at least a degree of acceptance in New Zealand when you're called a "bloody yank" to your face.

In addition to the monthly fees due to Crown Shipwrights, our contract provided for separate housing with all utilities paid and an expense-paid automobile for each of us.

A very fair agreement. We had only to pay for our food and entertainment.

Molly was hired as a maid at a motel located within walking distance of our house in Auckland. Her wages were sufficient to pay for our daily living expenses. This enabled us to save all of my earnings during the 14 months that we were involved with the project.

As a result of this team effort, we returned to Hawaii having recouped all of the money that we spent on the four-year circumnavigation, including *Swan*'s moorage fees while we were in New Zealand, and some to boot. We were walking in tall cotton.

About the time that the boatbuilding project was winding down, Doug and I made a business decision that we have since referred to in a wide range of terms. However, the passage of time has mellowed our memories of this "prize piece of business." I like to remember it as "The Great Double-Drum Sander Affair."

Standing in the corner of a lumber dealer's warehouse in Auckland was a huge, ancient, heavy cast-iron, double-drum sander. As you might have already guessed, it would have been in the best interests of the now international firm of Crown Shipwrights, Inc. if the sander were still standing in the corner of the Auckland warehouse. Unfortunately, it was for sale.

It was the grand idea that captivated us. A machine that could sand, dead flat, whole slabs of wood—doors—anything up to 36 inches wide and several inches thick. As far as we knew there wasn't a sander in all of Hawaii that could even come close to it. Of course we were basing this judgement on no research whatsoever. That is why "as far as we knew" is a valid statement.

After the usual polite dickering we paid the man $500 cash on the barrelhead for the lovely monstrosity. The fellow looked very relieved, it seemed to me. He asked us if we would be moving it soon. His question sort of dampened the euphoria we had been feeling about our acquisition. The moving thing was something that we knew was involved, but we hadn't fully ad-

28

dressed the problem. It was like having to move an elephant, only worse, because an elephant can walk.

When the foreman at the boatyard learned about our purchase he immediately offered us $1000 for it—double our money on the spot—as is/where is. Not a chance! His offer was solid confirmation of our business acumen. We never considered accepting it for an instant. We knew only too well the stories about the people that Henry Ford had approached, asking them to invest $500 in his machine. Some of those people, devoid of vision, had waffled and turned him down, missing the ride. We were not of that ilk. We had the vision. Entrepreneurial blood coursed through our veins. That hulking mass of cast-iron was headed for Hawaii on the next northbound freighter!

We spent a few days dismantling the sander and building a heavy timber skid for transporting it to Honolulu. It would be three months in transit—enough time for us to do the advance work.

When the 747's wheels touched down at Honolulu we were in great spirits. We had accomplished in less than two years what we had figured would take five. One thing we knew for sure, we were out of the boat business. The New Zealand project would be a tough act to follow. Working on boats in Honolulu amounted to grubbing around in bilges for the most part. Home repair and renovation seemed like the right direction for our company—and it would fit in with our sanding business.

Swan had managed to get along very well under Carson and Katy's care, and it was a joy to move back on board. For *Swan's* benefit we spoke disparagingly about the inefficiencies of living in a large rambling house. We were very careful not to mention the hot tub and laundry facilities.

The military had lifted their hiring freeze, and Molly was hired as a nurse at Tripler Army Hospital after the usual hassle one faces when dealing with a federal agency. It was well worth the effort. Her job paid well and the steady income easily met our living expenses and allowed me the latitude to pursue our business plans.

One of the first acts of the Board of Directors of Crown

Shipwrights, upon our return to Hawaii, was to change the corporate name to R&R Oahu, Inc. The R&R stood for Repair and Renovation. We intentionally wanted the name to be vague so we wouldn't be locked into one arena of enterprise. The name R&R Oahu gave rise to any number of interpretations, ranging from Rest & Recuperation to the more vicious Rip & Run.

We rented a tiny three-cornered, corrugated steel shed in the boatyard at Keehi. Our previous shop had been too large and expensive for the volume of business that we were doing. We had resolved not to make that mistake again. It was just possible that we had overcompensated a bit with our new location. We referred to the shed as The R&R Building or Corporate Headquarters.

Of the shed's many shortcomings, an affinity for moisture was its most glaring and miserable one. It welcomed water in any form, from any source, from any direction. It was the storm drain of Honolulu. When it rained, the floor would flood four inches deep. We placed concrete building blocks as stepping-stones with planks bridging the deep areas. Running an electrical power tool there was almost certainly a death sentence.

The flat roof leaked like a sieve. I climbed up there once to attempt to caulk the seams. The sight that greeted me was intimidating. It was covered with hundreds of beer cans that the guys in the fiberglass shop next door had been throwing up there for months. It was their way of keeping the cans from falling into the hands of the scavengers who prowled the yard early in the morning looking for cans. The cache of cans was their company's savings account.

In dry weather the shed was a furnace. It reminded me of the steel punishment box that the English Colonel was put in for days on end in the tropical sun in the movie "The Bridge on the River Kwai." If I had been confined by an enemy force in Corporate Headquarters for 15 minutes in the noonday sun, I would have given them the secret invasion plans in triplicate.

Getting started in the home improvement business was a struggle. Doug and I walked the streets of the up-scale neighborhoods knocking on doors and passing out handbills. The approach was mildly successful and we got some jobs, most of them menial, but after a few weeks we had gotten some referrals and R&R Oahu, Inc. was stumbling along in business.

One day a form letter arrived in the mail from the U.S. Customs Service. The sander had arrived. We needed only to sign some papers, pay some fees, and we could haul it away.

We rented a flatbed truck and drove to the docks. A sheaf of bureaucratic paperwork had accumulated with the two governments involved. When everything was in order, a forklift loaded the sander onto the truck and we transported our prize to the boatyard.

In order to make the sander as compact as possible for shipping, we had removed the bulky sheet metal guards and strapped them on top of the machine in any way that they would fit, giving it the appearance of a large stack of neatly packaged scrap metal. It drew plenty of onlookers and a lot of questions. "You shipped *that* all the way from New Zealand?" The most common question was: "What the hell is it?"

A forklift set the sander under the cover of a large open shed where the refurbishing would take place. Our plan was to work on the machine during slack periods in the home improvement business.

The sander had been built in England, at least a half century earlier, and had the name "Pickles" in embossed letters on the heavy cast base. We took it apart, checking for worn bushings and bearings, and thoroughly cleaned and greased the moving parts. It was in remarkably good condition. The three large electric motors that drove the sanding drums and conveyor feed belt were a different cycle than that used in the American electrical power system, and had to be replaced. This was not cheap.

The meter had been running steadily on this investment: the original purchase price, transportation in Auckland, surface shipping, dock fees at each end, U.S. Customs fees, the rental truck costs, the new electric motors, and several small expenditures. The bottom line had grown from the original $500 to approximately $3500.

All that remained was the cosmetic work. We cleaned the

base and housings with muriatic acid and painted the machine gloss white. All of the take-up wheels, levers, grease cups, and knobs were buffed and chrome plated. As a final touch I carefully painted the embossed letters "Pickles" bright red against the gleaming white. It was a splendid piece of machinery—phoenixlike—risen from the Auckland sawdust.

People paused to admire it. They were singing a different tune now. Perhaps it was time for yet another company name change, I mused. With our English machine and Hawaii's English heritage, we could advertise ourselves as: The Sanding Kings of the Sandwich Islands. A new and grand beginning—we had *the* machine.

Test day finally arrived. The drums were fitted with sandpaper, and the three electric motors were humming. Doug had scrounged up a rough plank that would soon be smooth. We were crouched at the feed end of the machine looking into the slot between the conveyor and the spinning drums. In my right hand I gripped the chrome lever that operated the conveyor table. It was smooth and solid-feeling like a lever ought to be.

Doug fed the timber onto the conveyor belt. "Bring it up a little," he said. I pulled back on the lever and the conveyor table rose slowly as we closely watched the gap closing.

"Bring it up some more—just a——" BOOM!

It was a thunderous noise—like a cannon. We stood dumbfounded. People came running. They thought a boat had fallen over.

The cast-iron sanding drum on the far side of the machine was *gone*, or most of it anyway. It was bolted together and had somehow flown apart at high speed.

A chunk weighing 65 pounds flew through the corrugated steel roof 18 feet above the floor, shearing a wooden beam in two, and carried over the washrooms, landing on the hood of a car in the parking lot.

A long cast-iron guide bar that weighed about 125 pounds sheared its mounting bolts, shot sideways through the machine shop wall, and smashed in the side of a row of steel lockers. Jagged shards of metal ranging from small bits to chunks the size of a softball hit a concrete block wall, leaving large pockmarks.

Doug and I walked across the yard, away from the scene. We couldn't believe we were still standing. The drum nearest us had deflected the blast. If that drum had been the one that exploded, there is little doubt that we would have been maimed or killed outright. Miraculously, no one was injured.

The days immediately following the blowup are vague in my memory. It was as if we had survived a plane crash and were having a hard time adjusting to the fact. When we recovered we discussed our possible alternatives vis-a-vis the sander. Doug had the right answer: salvage the motors and get it the hell out of here!

I made a deal with the yard supervisor. If he would take the sander to the scrapyard a few blocks away, he could have the proceeds from the sale. He agreed.

Nestled among my foggy recollections of the sander's demise is one memory that remains indelible in my mind. It is the scene of the gleaming white machine with the glint of the afternoon sun reflecting off its chromed cranks and levers, lurching down the potholed road on the forklift toward the scrapyard. It turned the corner and was gone forever.

In the fall of 1987 we put *Swan* up for sale. Our business was thriving and we had tentative plans to purchase a home and hang up the cruising anchor for good. Hawaii had been our home for six years and it seemed like the logical thing to do. But our hearts were not really into moving ashore; it would most likely close the book on cruising. We were having misgivings about the decision.

Early one morning as I was leaving for work I paused and looked back at *Swan* lying forlornly in her slip. Molly and I had never been happier than when we were sailing our valiant little ship, bound for some distant port. I turned and walked on toward the parking lot, then I paused again. In my mind's eye I saw the scene that had been recurring in my daydreams regularly for several months: *Swan* running before the wind through a sparkling blue ocean, with dolphins diving in twos and threes across the bow; sea birds swooping low over white-capped seas, and pure freedom stretching in all directions.

Cruising boats are for cruising, and *Swan* was a cruising

boat, and cruising was what we wanted to do. Then why were we thinking of selling her? I walked back to the boat and cut the For Sale sign down.

When Molly came aboard that night after working the evening shift at the hospital, she saw that I was still awake with a jug of wine and two glasses on the table. "Uh-oh," she said.

"No no," I said, pointing to a stack of charts on the chart table. "We're going cruising. We're outta here!"

She stood staring at me for a moment and said, "Can I take a shower first?"

This spark ignited the flame. Suddenly it was 1977 again. Charts all over the place—lists being made. It was probably my imagination but *Swan* appeared livelier—tugging at her lines.

We had a full agenda. During our years in Hawaii *Swan* had received only routine maintenance. She was 10 years old and she had put nearly 40,000 blue-water miles behind her. It was time for a stem-to-stern examination.

At this time I was working on my book manuscript: *By Way of the Wind*. Each morning, before leaving for work, I wrote in the cockpit by the light of a small reading lamp from 0500 until 0730. On the weekend I worked on the manuscript four to five hours each day. The book would require a minimum of one year to complete.

With all of this to do, we set our departure date for the spring of 1989. But where to go? For a time we considered making another circumnavigation, but after a while that idea lost its appeal. We had done that, and it seemed rather pointless to do it again.

Why not sail back to Oregon for the summer and then begin what would be, more or less, a circumnavigation of the United States via the Panama Canal, with a sojourn in the Sea of Cortez en route. Just let the voyage play out without a script—no final destination in mind, and no time limit—cruising in its purest form.

This voyage would give us a good measure of open-ocean cruising, with many ports of call along the way as a change of pace. It sounded like a winner to us. The matter was settled.

Swan spent a month hauled out in the boatyard about 50 yards from the new and improved Corporate Headquarters. The old punishment box had been torn down two years earlier, and we had moved into a proper-sized, well-ventilated shop. It was a rare convenience for a cruising sailor to have a boat hauled out with access to a well-equipped shop day and night.

The undersides of *Swan* were in excellent condition. Thirteen years in the water and there wasn't one blister. There were a few rust spots on the fin keel. I had the yard people sandblast it, then I faired it and painted it with four coats of epoxy paint.

My survey of the boat showed three problems that could not be ignored: questionable chainplates, the fuel tank had a rust problem, and the anchor windlass needed an overhaul.

The chainplates were integral to the hull and could not be completely examined, which is why they were questionable. To be safe we replaced all of them. This was not a simple matter.

With the mast standing throughout the job, I removed each chainplate, replaced it, and put it back in service before proceeding to the next one.

I cut the chainplates off beneath the surface of the fiberglass and repaired the damaged area. The new plates were made of low-carbon content 316L stainless steel (the letter "L" signifies low carbon). They were electropolished and bolted in place on the outside of the hull in a bedding of 3M brand 5200 caulking, a superior product that has stood the test of time in all of its applications on *Swan*.

Over the years I have seen many boats with what I believe are serious defects in the design of their chainplates. Most often these design defects have been on self-built boats, even though the builders, in most cases, tried to do the best possible job. The problem lies in the location of the hole drilled in the chainplate to accept the toggle pin, and the hole diameter.

The hole should be drilled as far below the top of the chainplate as the depth of the throat of the toggle will allow, without restricting its ability to pivot. This leaves the maximum amount of metal possible between the top edge of the hole and the top of the plate. The tendency is to drill the hole equidistant from the top and sides of the plate, creating a potential failure area directly above the pin (See Fig. 2).

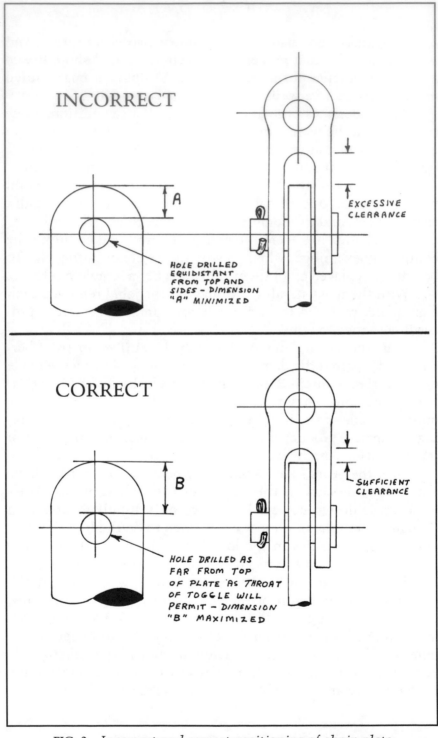

FIG. 2 *Incorrect and correct positioning of chain plate toggle pin hole*

Toggles are necessary to act as universal joints between the shrouds or stays and the chainplates when lateral as well as fore-and-aft movement is present in a seaway, or when a pronounced catenary is produced in a forestay by the sail. Toggles should *always* be used. However, when the rigging is set up tight, causing heavy pressure on the toggle pins, the pivoting action of the toggle can be greatly reduced, or even eliminated. When this is the case, the movement occurs in the chainplate hole, provided there is sufficient clearance for the pin to rock as well as pivot. If there isn't a small tolerance, the wire flexes and this usually leads to the strands breaking at the terminal hard spot. Also, the movement and vibration of the wire can be transferred to the chainplate, promoting metal fatigue.

I drilled the holes in the chain plates 3/32" larger than the toggle pins. When I twanged the taut rigging, with my hand on the toggle pin and the chainplate, I could feel the toggle moving, but almost no vibration could be detected in the chainplate itself.

It is a good idea to occasionally lubricate the turnbuckle toggle pins with a spray lubricant to help eliminate the sluggish pin problem. This is one of the things I did on long passages on my daily "walk around," which I will discuss later.

One of my recurring boat-associated nightmares is the one in which I relive the replacement of the fuel tank. I thoroughly cursed the imbecile that installed it until I remembered that I built the boat. Because it is not my intent to solicit pity, I will spare you the gruesome details. Suffice it to say that it was such a horrible experience that I went to great lengths, and spared no expense, to ensure that the new tank would outlast the pyramids, or survive me by 50 years, whichever came first, and that it would do nothing but hide beneath the cockpit sole and efficiently supply fuel to the engine forevermore.

Work hardening of the fuel pick-up tube is a potential problem area in fuel tanks. Many boats use copper tubing that is suspended free from a fitting on the top of the tank. The sloshing fuel causes a small movement of the tubing, which can eventually fatigue it and cause it to crack at the fitting.

To prevent this from happening while I was still on the planet, I drilled out a stainless steel nut equal to the outside di-

37

ameter of a heavy-walled bronze tube that was used for the fuel pick-up. The tube fit into the nut, which I welded to the bottom of the tank (See Fig. 3). A half-round slot was filed in the tube immediately above the nut, and this served as the fuel inlet port. The tube was held securely at the top and bottom, but it could be removed. As the intake port was slightly elevated, it precluded the possibility of picking up the last gallon of potentially impure fuel, should anyone be so careless as to run out of fuel. The dregs could be pumped out through the filler pipe.

Removing the anchor windlass paled in comparison to the fuel tank job, but it had its moments. While squeezed into the chain locker beating the five-inch, caulked in, windlass mounting bolts up through the deck, it dawned on me that putting the bolts in from the top, like nearly everyone does, is actually the wrong way from a practical viewpoint.

When I reinstalled the windlass, I used new bolts that were the correct length, and drove them up from the underside of the deck, which created four protruding studs. Neat-looking, self-locking nuts were used to fasten the windlass in place. The windlass can now be removed in minutes without disturbing the seal at the bolt holes.

Next came a ritual inspection for leaks. There are few boating miseries, other than chronic seasickness, that can transform a dream cruise into a nightmare as quickly as a hopelessly wet boat. We have seen boats arrive in port with every cushion in the boat sodden with salt water.

Swan has never leaked a drop, except for one time on a run down to the Equator when an unnamed skipper impulsively brought her around 180 degrees trying to retrieve a glass Japanese fishing ball and took a green sea over the bow, with a fair portion of it entering the wide-open forward hatch.

This incident has ever since proved to be an effective lever to counter any criticism that this skipper might occasionally direct at his First Mate for small oversights from time to time. It has always seemed a bit unfair when one considers that the skipper was intent on retrieving the float to adorn the garden beside the little cottage in the woods that he was going to build for his mate one day.

During the building of *Swan* we had subjected the deck fit-

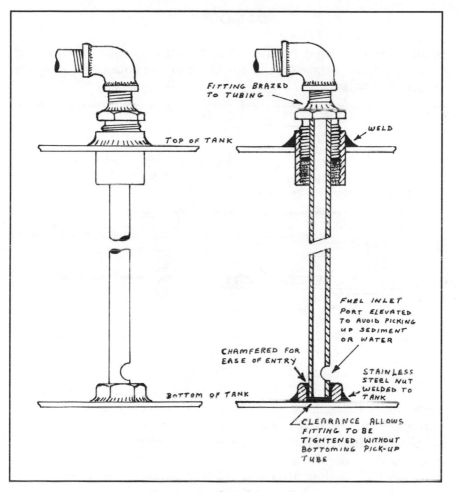

FIG. 3 *Fuel pick-up tube*

tings, cabin ports, forward hatch, and every potential leak area to a thorough water test using a garden hose with a high-pressure nozzle at *close range*. If one drop of water entered the boat, the faulty seal was reworked. The main companionway received a less stringent test because of its protection under the dodger and the impracticality of achieving perfect watertight integrity there.

Each bolt hole drilled in the deck for attachment of a fitting was countersunk to form an "O-ring" type seal of 3M 5200 caulking around the fastener (See Fig. 4). All bolts were tightened fully, without regard to the thickness of the bedding com-

39

pound between the deck surface and fitting, because the critical seal was made certain by the caulking in the countersunk space around the bolts.

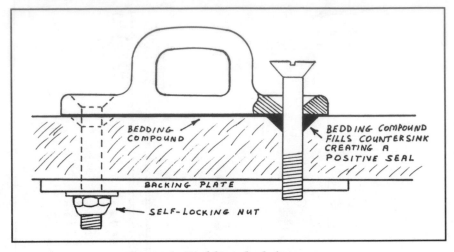

FIG. 4   *Bedding deck fittings*

Countless foredeck inundations by breaking seas in gales *Swan* has battled over the years have proven that if a sealing surface, joint, or fitting can pass the water test, it can be assumed that it will not leak at sea unless physical deterioration of the sealing agent occurs.

I was concerned that a decade of exposure to the tropical sun had deteriorated the caulking, so I subjected every potential leak source to the water test. There were no leaks.

In the first week of April 1989, Doug and I sat on a workbench in the R&R Building with a pencil and paper and a six-pack of beer. Before the beer was finished we had agreed on a fair price for my part of the business partnership that had grown more solid with each passing year.

We went across the road to a little waterfront restaurant to have lunch and tip a few. Doug picked up the check—after all, I was unemployed.

4

PROVISIONING THE BOAT FOR A VOYAGE is normally an ordeal that requires careful planning and many hours of shopping. Then everything must be dated and cataloged by category, or in some cases item by item, and stored away. But for this passage to the mainland, provisioning was a simple matter. We were sailing to where the provisions came from, so we were traveling light. No point in carrying coals to Newcastle.

On the morning after an outstanding Aloha party given for us by our friends, we sailed out of Honolulu on an overnight run to Hanalei Bay on the north shore of Kauai. This diversion across the Kauai Channel allowed us to become at least partially acclimated to the rugged conditions that awaited us on the first leg of the passage to Oregon; a 500-mile northerly slog through the Northeast Trades.

It also gave us an opportunity to put off biting the bullet— a little procrastination that would set the tone for this open-ended voyage. Besides, one doesn't need a special reason for wanting to visit the beautiful bay where Puff the Magic Dragon lives.

It was encouraging that neither of us felt the slightest trace of seasickness, even though the channel was fairly rough. My occasional bouts with seasickness had almost always been the result of early morning departures after Aloha parties where I concentrated too much on the spirits *at* the party, rather than the spirit *of* the party. I had been reasonably temperate at our going-away blast. The old seadog was learning.

Satellite navigation receivers had finally gotten down to an affordable price and we had purchased one for this voyage. It was our first opportunity to test it other than at the dock. There was no doubt that it would be a great aid to navigation, but I have an abiding distrust for electronics, and I had promised myself that if possible, the SatNav would be kept honest with at least one confirming celestial LOP each day.

Bearings on landmarks taken during the channel crossing confirmed the accuracy of the instrument, and it was reassuring to have it update our position every 40 minutes or so during the night.

Our excitement about leaving, coupled with adjusting to bunks that for seven years had been restful retreats, but had suddenly been transformed by the bumpy channel into jostling places, prevented us from getting more than a few catnaps during the 24-hour run to Hanalei.

This was part of the reason for our stop at the bay. We had made only one inter-island sailing trip and a few Sunday afternoon sails to Waikiki during the entire time that we lived in Honolulu. A few days at anchor would wean us away from any landlubberly habits and routines that had crept insidiously into our lives during the years spent at the dock, and help ease us back into the cruising mode.

At daybreak we were running along the north shore of Kauai, escorted by a playful group of dolphins. They stayed with us for about three miles and exuberantly led the way into Hanalei Bay. No doubt they were friends of Puff.

Our brief stop stretched into a week, which we spent swimming, diving, and generally putting off the first leg of the passage. Each day I looked northward with binoculars, and each day it was the same: white horses stretching into infinity. There was no point in waiting any longer. The laws of nature were not likely to change. It was time to go.

One last walk to a nearby village to buy fresh vegetables and we were ready. We brought the dinghy on board and broke the anchor loose from the seductive sands of Hanalei Bay. Molly had her battered Brer Bear hat on. That meant business!

Getting out of the Northeast Trades as comfortably as possible was our primary concern. If it took three days or six days it really didn't matter. Thrashing and bashing closehauled against the trades wasn't in our rule book. Our strategy was the same as it had been when we made this passage earlier. We hanked on the working jib and storm trysail, set the vane on a close reach on the starboard tack, trimmed the sails, and let her go.

A close reach was a fast point of sail that we could easily tolerate, and it was not too hard on the gear. It didn't matter a whit if we made a mile of easting. If the trades moved eastward—great! If they backed to the north, that wasn't so great, but we would still be moving northward.

The irony of the situation was that *north* of 30°N was now the promised land. In a very general sense, 30°N was the southern boundary of a 10-degree belt of variable winds and easterly setting currents, through which a sailing vessel could make up to the northeastward into the 40s where the prevailing westerlies blew.

Ten hours out and the SatNav informed us that we were slipping to the westward. It also provided us with the heartening fact that we had made 60 miles good—a spirited six knots under reduced sail. I wasn't accustomed to having such precise navigational information at my fingertips, and I wasn't really sure how I was going to adjust to this smart-aleck navigator who could see in the dark.

Molly and I have a tendency to humanize equipment that performs functions normally carried out by humans; a penchant that accounted for Vane's elevated status on board. We were already referring to the SatNav as "Cool Navigator," a takeoff from some '50s song. I conjured up a scene in my mind of imperious Vane taking his steering headings directly from Cool Navigator while I stood off to the side gazing through the sextant like some relic from the past.

At noon on the second day, 51 hours into the passage, we were 290 miles north of Kauai and had lost just 30 minutes of longitude to the west. I was elated with such excellent progress. We had literally not touched a sail or sheet since we trimmed them when we cleared the entrance of Hanalei Bay, and we'd made only occasional steering refinements to the trim of the tiller and the steering vane. *Swan* was driving north in steady Force 5 winds without help from anyone.

Eleven years in the tropics had eroded away what little tolerance Molly had for cool weather. It was early May and the nights were crisp. She had unearthed the New Zealand wool blankets when Kauai was still visible in the rearview mirror.

At 1630 on the evening of the third day, near 29°N, we decided to treat ourselves to a Sundowner and a civilized supper. This could not realistically happen with *Swan* bounding along at six knots in 10-foot seas.

I close-hauled the jib and unfastened the vang from the port toerail. Molly brought the bow through the eye of the wind, backwinding the jib, and the boom came across to the starboard side in the close-reach position, which was the proper trim for heaving-to when the trysail was paired with the working jib. I attached the vang to the starboard toerail and hauled the boom down hard to eliminate any movement. Molly put the helm down (to leeward) and lashed it in that position. That was all there was to it—we were hove-to on the port tack.

The instant change in a boat's motion when she is hove-to in a seaway always intrigues me. Suddenly it is almost tranquil, where a minute before the boat was pitching and driving through the seas. The boat heels and makes leeway in a nearly square drift, with the forward drive of the trysail or reefed mainsail countered by the backwinded jib. If they are trimmed properly, the battle of the sails is almost imperceptible. The main drives the boat slowly ahead and the rudder brings the bow up on the wind until the main is on the verge of luffing, losing its driving force. At this point the backed jib overpowers the main; the boat loses headway and falls off until the wind pressure on the main begins to drive it forward—and the cycle is repeated (See Fig. 5).

The rolling motion of the boat is nearly eliminated by the constant wind pressure on the backed jib. Because of the angle of heel, the turn of the bilge is presented to the seas, reducing the impact of the waves on the hull. They don't crash against the hullsides as one might expect—only a surge is felt as the seas, broad on the bow, pass obliquely beneath the boat.

The term "heave-to" generally connotes an option one has in managing a boat in a storm offshore. But there are many other instances when the capacity of a boat to achieve this remarkable state of relative calm can be of great value to the crew of a blue-water cruising boat. A few of these are: to make a repair; to treat a wound; to give a seasick person an opportunity to recover; to get a few hours of rest; to wait for dawn to enter a port; to wait for an opportunity to fix one's position when sailing in hazardous waters; or just to take a break from a tiring windward slog.

It is a tactic that can be practiced on a windy day in one's home waters. It doesn't have to be in gale force winds. *Swan* assumed the same attitude to the seas and behaved essentially the same in 20 knots of wind as she did in a gale of wind if the appropriate sails were used. Different sails can be tried until the right combination is found for the particular boat design.

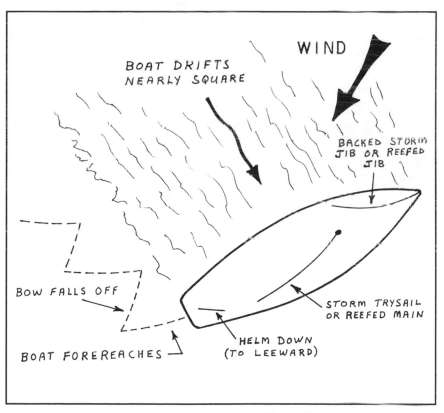

FIG. 5 *Heaving-to under sail*

We had practiced heaving-to before we set out as pollywog sailors on our first ocean passage—but it was just one of many things learned during a relatively short period, and the maneuver wasn't exactly second nature to me.

This fact came home vividly when we found ourselves in deteriorating weather 30 miles off the coast of California. We had left port in conditions that were better suited to having a few beers and shooting pool in the marina pub than sailing boats. The upshot of my knot-headed decision to leave was that we were soon in the middle of a building gale, dead on the nose, and night was falling. We were totally exhausted and making no headway worth mentioning in the dangerous short-period seas. We needed to heave-to before something drastic happened.

Admiral Sir Francis Beaufort apparently devised his scale of wind without any graphic input from fledgling sailors who had been caught in a gale in the dark of night on their maiden voyage in a 36-foot sailboat. If he had, all of his most horrifying descriptions of the sea state would have been used up by the time he got to Force 9.

I was so numbingly tired that I was having difficulty recalling what we were supposed to do first when heaving-to. Huddled under the dodger with a flashlight, I refreshed my memory by reading aloud to the mate the section on heaving-to in the "How To Sail" book. I vividly emphasized the dire consequences that would befall us if we failed to comply with the exact letter of the instructions.

At this embryonic stage of our cruising life Molly had an almost blind faith in my judgment. She hung on my every word as I read the book in a loud voice over the howling gale, like a fire and brimstone evangelist reading the Word to his flock of one.

Molly still has faith in me, but it isn't the blank check that it once was.

The crux of my condensed interpretation of the book's message was that if we didn't do something pretty quick, other than what we were doing, we were going to die.

We followed the "Five Easy Steps To Heaving-To," and

hove-to with the trysail and storm jib. Not once did a sea break aboard during the course of many hours that we weathered the gale in relative comfort and safety. Heaving-to became a valuable staple in our inventory of cruising tactics.

Now to get back to the cocktail hour.

Hove-to on the port tack, *Swan*'s bow assumed an attitude of about 50 degrees off the wind, pointed east-southeast. Molly opened one of the windward cabin ports and let the wind blow briskly through the boat without a trace of spray while she cooked supper.

I poured several buckets of seawater in the cockpit to wash away the accumulated salt residue and wiped it down with a chamois.

We sat in the cockpit drinking a glass of wine and enjoying the warmth of the late afternoon sun. Around us the seas rolled relentlessly toward the southwest, and the wind whistled over the dodger. We were strangely like spectators, rather than participants in the scene. This was the cruising equivalent of stopping to smell the roses.

While the mate squared away the galley, I took the opportunity to do a "walk around" on deck without the encumbrance of a safety harness. Checking for chafe and any signs of rigging problems were my primary concern. I had long ago discarded the plastic tubes that once covered the turnbuckles. They discouraged inspection and maintenance of the fittings. On this tour of the forward area I found nothing out of order.

I always carried a can of silicone spray lubricant on these inspections. I sprayed the turnbuckle toggles and the mainsail track as far up as I could reach, and gave the whisker pole's spring-loaded pins a shot.

Cool Navigator (hereinafter called CN) was a workaholic and had produced two fixes during the 90-minute stop. His little fix-alert diode was frantically flashing so that we would be aware that our dalliance in the sun had cost us nearly two miles of leeward drift.

As the sun neared the horizon we took a cockpit bath before getting on with the passage. Mentally and physically re-

freshed by this pleasant interlude, we put the helm to windward, allowing the bow to fall off the wind. The boat wore
around in a clockwise circle; the main jibed, and the sails filled
on the starboard tack. I eased the jib a bit and reset the vang.
Swan resumed her northerly course.

There probably isn't such a thing as a good watch system
for two people on a cruising boat making an ocean passage.
Some systems are perhaps more tolerable than others—but
none is *good*.

When a person is required to climb out of a warm, comfortable bunk from a sound sleep in the middle of the night,
pull on his clothes and fumble with a safety harness; then go
up on deck to squint over the dodger between blasts of cold salt
water looking for lumbering, yacht-smashing hulks—it ain't
good!

After having completed 34 ocean passages, I don't believe
that I could write a coherent paragraph on our watch system, if
one could call it that.

Generally, I slept from about 2000 until the mate began
looking cross-eyed. This usually occurred sometime between
2400 and 0130. She would wake me, then let me sleep for another 15 minutes because I always acted so pitiful that it would
bring out the mother instinct in her.

She would then inform me of the average speed we had
made on her watch, remind me of the course, hand me my
safety harness, and climb into our mutual bunk, where she
slept until about 0700.

I would sit on the settee with my safety harness dangling
between my knees, staring into the darkness and listening to
the rush of the water on the hull for about 10 minutes. Finally, I would go up on deck and scan the horizon for ships
and check the set of the sails with a flashlight before enscons-
ing myself in the leeward corner of the cockpit under the
dodger.

I looked at the compass about once an hour. The rest of
the time, on clear nights, I used a star in relation to one of the
backstays as a course guide, and periodically selected a new
one as the heavens changed. The compass was mounted on

the bulkhead, and to see it I would be forced to move the cushion I was leaning against, which was a bloody nuisance.

I normally passed the nights reading by a small red light, checking the horizon every 10 or 15 minutes, and dozing off and on; but always with a timer set, which I advanced continually. At daybreak I put the trolling lines out and set the alarm for a 30-minute nap in the cockpit.

This was our "watch system." So far the U.S. Naval Academy has not expressed an interest in knowing more about it.

At noon on the fourth day of the passage we were 510 miles north of Kauai and had made three degrees of easting. We couldn't have hoped for a better run out of the trades. They held steady until we reached 31°N and then faded away.

For a short time Vane took us on a eastward odyssey, following a fickle southerly breeze that had replaced the robust trades. Then the wind shifted to the southeast and freshened. We took in the jib and hanked on the reacher, leaving the trysail in place.

A fairer wind never existed. For seven days it held nearly steady from the southeast, squarely on the beam. During this period we sailed 895 miles, averaging 5.32 knots. Our course was dead at the mouth of the Columbia River, which lay 1800 miles northeast of our position at the start of the seven day run.

It was truly a dream sail. We flew the reacher for the entire seven days—one headsail change since our departure from Kauai!

Swan marked off the miles at a good speed, flying the reacher and trysail combination with little danger of the boat being suddenly overpowered. We never flew the full main with the reacher at night, except in rare instances when we were both awake in calm weather.

It is a traumatic experience indeed to be awakened by a cry from the person on watch to find the boat heeled over heavily, rounding up, and generally out of control in the midst of a violent squall.

It took about two times on our early passages of rushing on deck in the dark, half dressed, to fight down large sails, often in a torrent of rain and blasting spray, for me to understand the foolishness of a shorthanded crew flying full canvas during the night watch. We had evolved into conservative sailors.

We had met more than one lonely macho sailor whose first mistake had been sailing recklessly across the ocean at top speed, through tempest and turbulence, to some distant island in the sun, accompanied by his gentle and frightened mate— and whose second mistake was not knowing there was an airport on the island.

CN was pumping out fixes at a prodigious rate. During the run up through the trades I had taken the noon latitude each day to verify his fixes. The latitudes coincided with the positions, so I assumed the longitude was correct also. The fixes agreed with my estimated position (EP), and there wasn't anything that we could hit for thousands of miles anyway. But to be sure, I took a round of star sights which further confirmed CN's talents.

On this splendid seven-day sleighride, Vane steered, CN navigated, and the sails remained untouched until the fifth day of the run when the wind increased in force. We took down the trysail and ran under the reacher alone, logging 156 miles for that day.

It was on my watch in the middle of the night that our ersatz tradewind began to run out of steam. One becomes attuned to the sounds and the motion of a boat underway. A two-degree variation in the angle of heel, or the difference in sound that an increase or decrease of one knot of boatspeed makes as the bow cuts through the water, signals a change in the velocity of the wind. I detected a subtle diminution of the driving force of the boat. I had a feeling that the party would soon be over.

Over was certainly the word for it! For 17 hours we lay dead in the water. Dead, in the sense of not moving forward. There was plenty of boat movement in the running sea, but it had nothing to do with progress. That was when Molly heard the sound of water sloshing in the bilge.

There are few things more disconcerting on board a boat far out to sea than the sight of water in a bilge that is supposed to be dusty dry. The level of the water wasn't high enough to activate the bilge pump.

I tasted the water and it was salty, but not a heavy brine. Molly filled a glass with seawater from the galley pump. It tasted saltier than the water in the bilge, so I immediately suspected a leak in one of the freshwater tanks.

The brackish taste of the water could be attributed to the fact that twice each year for 10 years we had flooded the bilge with seawater to the level of the floorboards and let it stand for 24 hours. This permeated the wooden stringers with salt. I had borrowed the idea from the old sailing ships that had rock-salt shelves underneath the deck at the hull which turned leaking rainwater into brine to prevent rot. *Swan*'s stringers did not treat rot spores kindly.

A leak in the 83-gallon freshwater tank in the forepeak would be obvious, because the water would have to enter the bilge at the stem area aft of the tank, and this area was dry. After a long search I found the leak. It was in the 45-gallon polypropylene tank amidships. There was a tiny crack at an inaccessible spot (of course). It was a very slow leak.

Slow or not, Molly wanted something done about it. She could scarcely abide a dropping water level in the tanks from prudent use—a leak was intolerable. "It's leaking," she said. "It's got to be fixed!"

I explained that we had less than 900 miles to go, and the leak was small and getting smaller as the pressure decreased with the descending level of the water in the tank. I then added, rather undiplomatically given the mate's hydrophilic nature, that including the jerry jugs of emergency water, we had enough water on board to drown the Chinese Army.

The mate ignored this last piece of hyperbole and repeated, "It's leaking, it's got to be fixed!"

There was more to it than just saving the water. The water in the leaking tank, which was used for drinking and cooking, passed through a filter that removed the chlorine we had added to prevent algae growth. The larger forward tank was used for bathing and rinsing dishes and was not filtered. It was used at a faster rate than the amidships tank.

I transferred some of the water from the leaking tank to the forward tank and performed a little plumbing sleight-of-hand that allowed us to wash with the drinking water and drink the wash water. Peace and harmony were restored.

After several interminable hours the seas calmed down enough that we were able to get a few hours of fitful rest. At daybreak I started the iron spinnaker and we motored for three hours due east, which put the swells on the starboard bow, easing the tiresome rolling considerably.

Fishing had been uncommonly poor during this passage. We had caught one puny skipjack and released it. As we motored on this chilly morning with both trolling lines out, I noticed a large concentration of birds in a frenzy several hundred yards to the southeast.

We had never been very successful in our efforts to find fish. We caught them fairly regularly by pure chance, but this morning was an exception. I powered into the swells until we reached the swarm of screaming, diving birds.

Snap! Snap! There were two fish on. "We've got breakfast!" I shouted to Molly. This brought her on deck in a hurry. A few minutes later two fat albacore, the best-tasting tuna in our estimation, were lying in the cockpit.

Molly held the easterly course while I cleaned the fish. I filleted one and froze the other one whole for a barbecue that I was sure we would have with our friends, Chuck and Florence Schmiel, in Portland. We would never sail into Portland without at least one fish in the freezer, even if we had to buy one in Astoria.

Our breakfast that morning was one of my favorites: steamed/fried albacore, grits cooked with chopped onion and bell pepper (dried in this case), and a batch of the mate's "famous" stove-top biscuits.

Molly's best fish recipe involves a hybrid process of steaming and frying. It lends itself well to cooking on a boat. Her recipe, for cooking fish—any and all:

> Spread a thin coating of mayonnaise on both sides
> of the fillets and lightly salt. Sauté thin onion slices

in 2 tablespoons of butter or margarine with minced ginger (optional) prior to cooking fish, because the fish cooks quickly. Place fillets in a skillet and squeeze one-half teaspoon lemon or lime juice on each piece; more if "fishy" fish. Add one-fourth cup water and cover. Cook on medium heat until fish begins to flake apart. Turn once and cook on low heat until *just* cooked through. Overcooking fish is grounds for mutinous action. Rice goes well with this dish.

When our 17-hour dues had been paid, the wind came gently from the southwest. We ignored it for 15 or 20 minutes before getting underway. Too many times in the past we had rushed up on deck and raised the sails for a glorified catspaw that was masquerading as a bona fide wind.

We sailed a northerly course, 20 degrees off the rhumbline, putting the wind forward of the port quarter to keep the reacher filled. If the wind held we would pole out the headsail.

After four hours it was apparent that the wind wasn't a fluke. Mares' tails filled the southern sky. It was a solid wind. We had lucked out again.

Through trial and error we had developed a procedure for setting the whisker pole with little risk of injury, or the chance of being catapulted off the boat by a flogging sail in a seaway. As when setting up the doldrums sail, the pole was rigged in precise order:

Vane was set to steer downwind under bare poles. This was very important. It put the waves squarely astern, eliminating the corkscrew effect of quartering seas that made working on deck difficult.

We never handled the pole and sail together. Before we raised the sail, which was secured at the bow with shock cord, the pole was hoisted and guyed in its approximate sailing position, then the sail was raised. This procedure was accomplished in the following order: the working sheet was reeved through the outer jaw of the pole and led through a toerail block to the sheet winch. The pole-lift and foreguy were fastened to their respective bridles, with the inboard jaw of the pole snapped to the sliding car on the mast. The car was at the bottom of its track, at the level of the lifelines. This kept the pole fairly horizontal, preventing it from dipping into the sea. I then hoisted the pole to its approximate working position, slid the mast car to the top of the track, and adjusted the foreguy. The pole was now held in place by the pole-lift, the foreguy, and the loosely tensioned reacher sheet.

At this point I passed the sail over the lifeline while Molly hauled in the sheet until the clew of the sail was hard against the jaw of the pole. I then raised the sail and fine-tuned the running rigging. To douse the sail we reversed the process.

With everything in place we resumed our original course, but made no effort to close with the rhumbline.

I have found that many skippers seem compelled to return to the rhumbline when making an ocean passage, if for some reason the boat has sailed off course. For some, it's as if that imaginary line is akin to the Holy Grail.

If the boat has strayed, or has been forced off the rhumbline, and there is no reason to maintain a prescribed course, such as when sailing in proximity of reefs or shoal water, or running along a coast, a new course should be laid out. The old one is history. It was only relevant at your departure point, or for as long as you were sailing along it.

Each day, in mid-ocean, I calculated the new course as if the boat were created on the spot that it occupied at the moment of the fix. Obviously, as the vessel nears its destination one must maintain a more disciplined course.

On the morning of the 18th day of the passage we were 440 miles from the Columbia River outer marker—a three-day sail at best. The tide table showed low slack water at 0830 on Day 21, a good time to cross the bar. With a loss of one hour on the time change from Zone 9 to 8, we had exactly 72 hours. We would have to average 145 miles per day—a tall order—but wouldn't it be nice!

The southwest wind had shifted 90 degrees and was blowing at a solid Force 5 from the southeast, a perfect direction for our 055 True course. In character with our good luck on this passage, the wind held steady.

The dawning of the 21st day revealed Oregon's coastal mountain range, blue-gray in the morning haze. We were 20 miles from the river entrance. At 0800 we arrived at the outer marker. We never took *Swan* off self-steering until we were halfway across the bar. That's enough to spoil you rotten.

5

THERE IS SOMETHING THERAPEUTIC about washing accumulated salt off a boat with fresh water after an ocean passage. Especially when one is using Oregon water, which is soft and
superb. *Swan* deserved the finest treatment—once again she
had borne us safely across a great expanse of ocean. We arrived
rested and dry, with the only equipment failure being the slow
leak in the water tank.

Astoria is a perfect-sized town for a visiting yacht. Everything is within walking distance. There are nice places to eat
and small, crowded taverns near the marina. It is of sufficient
size to provide services, but not large enough to have lost its
small-town friendliness.

We celebrated the completion of the crossing with a night
on the town. The 2407-mile passage had taken 21 days, 3
hours, for an average speed of 4.75 knots. Running the engine
one hour each day to charge the system had consumed a whopping seven gallons of fuel, leaving us with 53 gallons on
board—General Motors should know our miles-per-gallon secret.

None of our friends or family had the slightest idea when
we were due to arrive. We had told them that we would be in
Portland sometime during the summer. That was as close to an
ETA as we cared to get.

Filing a float plan may be the perfectly correct thing to do
in some instances; however, we believe it is a mistake, by and
large, for long-distance cruising sailors to file one. Having to be
somewhere on or before a specific date is one of the regimenta-
tions of the workaday world that most cruisers whom we have

met were trying to escape. It precludes a spontaneous change in itinerary, or an extended stay at some charming spot unless the expectant party can be notified.

In my opinion, the minimal increase in risk this creates is a fair trade-off for the freedom from schedules, and the knowledge that a search plane isn't scouring the ocean looking for us because we dawdled along the way.

Another area where we did not conform to accepted practice was in our approach to survival gear, specifically the inflatable liferaft.

One of the first books we read when we decided to build a boat and go cruising was Dougal Robertson's fine book, *Survive The Savage Sea*. It made a lasting impression on us. The key to the Robertsons' survival after their boat sank was their ability to move. They owed their lives to a small sailing dinghy and a seaman's resourcefulness.

The idea of languishing impotently in an inflated doughnut at the total mercy of the current and capricious winds while waiting to be found was abhorrent to us. We dismissed the conventional liferaft from consideration and focused on finding a dinghy that would do double duty as transportation to and from the boat, and as a survival craft that would not puncture.

We settled on a seven-foot fiberglass sailing dinghy that was equipped with foam filled flotation chambers, a swing-down centerboard, rudder, and a free-standing mast made of aluminum.

I shortened the mast and fit it with a crosstree from which a small square-sail could be flown. A line led from the port and starboard corners of the transom to the respective ends of the crosstree. In addition to acting as stays, these lines supported a fitted cover that served as an awning, a rain catcher, and as a spray dodger.

The thought of being in a small open boat at sea was intimidating, but Mr. Robertson and crew did it, and Captain Bligh sailed an overloaded open boat for thousands of miles, keeping the stern to the wind and waves. It could be done.

In a stopwatch test, we launched the dinghy from an upside-down secured position in its chocks, to floating beside the boat, in 35 seconds. In an actual emergency it would probably have been faster because I would have cut the securing lines, we wouldn't have been concerned with marring the topsides, and we would have been scared as hell.

A rubberized, zippered duffel bag was fastened under the seat on each side of the centerboard trunk, with the zippered side facing the bottom of the dinghy. The bags held the survival gear. When the dinghy was in its normal position on deck, upside down in its chocks, the bags were high and dry with the zipper openings at the top.

Most of the contents of the bags were stored in double-packaged, pressure-sealed plastic bags with silica gel drier. The bags of small items were placed in wide-mouthed plastic jars with plastic lids. The jars had passed a submerged integrity test in three feet of water.

The following is a list of the contents in the bags:

——flare gun, 12 cartridges, 2 parachute flares, 2 smoke flares, 2 hand-held flares, dye marker, stainless steel signalling mirror.

——EPIRB

——liquid-filled hiker's compass, plastic sextant, plastic-coated waterproof table of average declinations of the sun for a year, with the back of the card blank for writing on with a water-soluble felt pen

——waterproof time and date quartz watch

——pencil and pad of paper

——stainless steel multi-purpose knife

——flashlight with O-ring-sealed switch and spare batteries

——butane lighter

——long-nose pliers

——assorted fish hooks, lures, line, lead weights, jar of fish eggs for chum or bait, Hawaiian Sling (a three-pronged fish spear with rubber lanyard—a very valuable piece of equipment)

——one 100% wool blanket

——two pairs long underwear—60% polyester for quick drying

——2 canvas brimmed hats with chin ties

——20 x 12-ounce cans purified drinking water (a five-gallon jug of water was kept on deck with a lanyard attached for abandoning ship)
——2 x seven-day Coast Guard-approved canned food rations
——sun operated saltwater still
——air mattress - when partially inflated it served as a cushion and back rest if lying in bottom of dinghy
——first-aid kit: assorted bandages and tape, steri strips, antibiotic ointment, crushable one-dose ampules of iodine, Valium tablets, aspirin, Tylenol-3, laxative, small scissors, tweezers, and needle
——2 pair polarized sunglasses
——sunscreen lotion
——5' x 7' vinyl tarp
——small roll of duct tape
——assortment of small nylon line
——bucket bailer
——plastic flask of rum
——deck of cards (be serious!)

I tested the dinghy rigged as a lifeboat in 20 knots of wind in Keehi Lagoon. It performed very well from a beam reach to downwind. That covered half the compass rose. The contraption resembled a seagoing covered wagon.

In my heart I had serious doubts about the value of our lifeboat or any liferaft in storm conditions. *Swan* was built so solidly, and her hull was laid up so well, that a storm that was capable of sinking her would have to be so severe that launching a small craft and getting aboard it would be an incredible feat in itself. If we managed to accomplish this, we would then have to survive the storm that sank *Swan* in a small boat. It all seemed unlikely.

But it would have been brash and foolish not to be prepared, and there are, of course, other reasons why boats sink besides storms.

I viewed making an ocean passage in *Swan* in the same way that I regarded flying in an airplane. Who would consider flying in an airliner if there was a special concern that it might crash? There is always a chance that an airliner might crash, but it is infinitesimal.

From the outset I felt that a great emphasis should be placed on constructing a boat so seaworthy that it would be as safe to sail it across an ocean as to fly across the same body of water in an airliner. Given all of the variables involved, that was a pretty lofty goal, but that is what we endeavored to do.

Having done our best, we then relegated the sickening specter of *Swan* disappearing beneath the stormy seas to the remote corner of our minds reserved for other unthinkable thoughts like a nuclear war, terminal cancer, and April 15th.

Before leaving the subject of safety and survival, I want to discuss a few random and time-proven design features, innovations, and maintenance routines that contributed to *Swan's* seaworthiness; some of which may be useful to you.

The design of the cockpit does not compromise the integrity of the boat, which is often the case with production boats. The companionway sill is elevated a few inches above the level of the seats. A sizeable quantity of water must flood the cockpit before it can enter the cabin.

Boats with companionway sills a few inches above the cockpit sole, fitted with slide boards, are at risk of flooding if the boat is knocked down or pooped. If I were cruising in a boat with a companionway designed in that manner, I would put the bottom slides in place to at least the level of the seats and fasten the top retaining slide securely in place with screws during the passage.

At the aft end of the cockpit I installed a four-inch drain that emptied straight out at the waterline. In a test at the dock it drained 66 gallons of water from the cockpit in 22 seconds. Two years later it came into play in a serious way when we were knocked down in the Tasman Sea with water flooding over the coaming like a waterfall. The drain more than earned its keep on that stormy, frightening night.

A little math reminder: one four-inch drain is equivalent in volume to four two-inch drains.

All of *Swan's* critical hose connections and the stuffing box coupling were double clamped with stainless steel hoseclamps. This is a fairly standard procedure in boatbuilding. What also seems to be fairly standard in the boating world is the dearth of attention the clamps receive once they are installed. Out of sight, out of mind.

I believe that some of this complacency stems from too much credence being given to the term "stainless steel." There is a great deal of boat equipment on the market that is manufactured with grades of stainless steel that would be more accurately described as "stains less steel." A large percentage of marine hoseclamps are of the "stains less" variety. There are superior grades of clamps available, but they are not always easy to find.

At two-year intervals I changed every hoseclamp that had the potential to sink the boat. I periodically sprayed them with a heavy silicone lubricant as scheduled maintenance.

In one test we conducted on a skeptic's boat, four out of nine critical stainless steel clamps snapped with normal screwdriver pressure. Tiny hairline rust cracks often develop in the band if the clamp is exposed to a saltwater environment.

Last on my worry list is propane fuel. A poorly installed and maintained propane system can be an explosive argument for a liferaft.

Generally speaking, maintenance of a propane system entails making occasional inspections of the propane tanks and lines, and keeping the tank and regulator fittings clean. There is little to go wrong with a properly installed system. Once each year we plugged the overboard drains in the propane locker and filled it with water to check for leaks belowdecks.

The approved rubber tubing used to supply propane to the consuming appliance has a bursting strength several times greater than the pressure of raw, unregulated propane, even at elevated tropical temperatures. I attempted to install the tubing in a way that would protect it from chafing or accidental damage.

I ran the propane tubing inside semi-rigid PVC pipe, supporting it along the sheer lamp at ten-inch intervals with rubber-lined hangers. A two-foot length of flexible propane hose connected the feed line to the stove, which was swung on a fore-and-aft axis. (A piece of yachting trivia: the widely used term "gimballed range" is a misnomer when applied to galley stoves that are hung on fore-and-aft pivots and swing athwartships only.)

The method used to support each end of the flexible hose is critical to its safe function and serviceable life. Typically, a bracket is fabricated that clamps the brass fitting of the flexible hose to a bulkhead at the supply end; and at the stove end, the hose fitting is screwed into a pipe fitting with no additional support. This is a very poor practice. It creates two hard spots which are potential failure points where the rubber tubing connects to the brass end fittings. Where does a garden hose rupture most frequently? At the hydrant fitting.

To prevent this from happening, I wrapped sheet rubber around the first few inches of the hose at each end and made brackets that clamped the rubber sleeves in place. This eliminated the hard spots and caused the hose to flex along its entire length (See Fig. 6).

My first inclination was to install an electrically operated solenoid valve at the tank to turn the gas on and off. Then I remembered what spark plugs do to engine cylinders full of explosive vapors. The solenoid valves were purported to be reliable and safe, but so was the Hindenburg. We turned the valves on and off at the tanks manually.

A final note on propane safety. I have read books and articles advocating the practice of shutting the propane supply off at the tank to allow the fuel to burn out of the supply line. In my opinion, this habit is unnecessary and dangerous. First, there is not enough propane in the line on an average size cruising boat to be concerned about, and second, it invites the possibility of leaving the burner on when the flame burns out. This could have dire consequences if the gas were turned on with no one below, or worse still, with a sound sleeper in the cabin.

Swan's mileage tally clicked over the 42,000 mark on the 80-mile motoring trip up the Columbia River. We meandered through the sloughs that branch off that mighty river, stopping at small towns, and gunkholing our way to Portland.

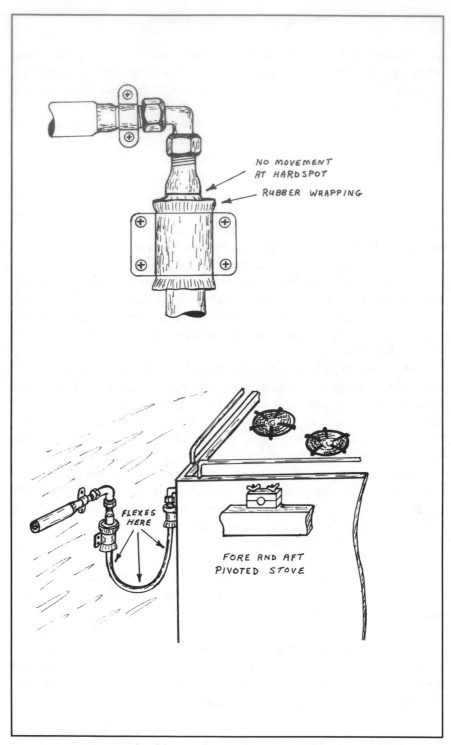

NO MOVEMENT
AT HARDSPOT

RUBBER WRAPPING

FLEXES
HERE

FORE AND AFT
PIVOTED STOVE

FIG. 6   *Propane feed hose clamped to prevent rupture at fitting*

My attention was focused on the diesel engine's less-than-sterling performance during the four-day run. It was suffering the long-term ill effects of having sucked great quantities of the Coral Sea into its innards on our earlier voyage. This unhealthy, even suicidal craving for salt water had exacted a heavy toll on its vital parts.

It was rather disconcerting how the aging diesel's decline mirrored my own advancing years. It had suffered a loss of power; it consumed more and accomplished less; more and more money had to be spent to keep it operating; and it was becoming obsolete.

Smoking was one thing I did not have in common with the engine. This was the most glaring of its problems. We could live with the loss of power; it wasn't too important whether we motored at five knots or six knots. The smoke was another matter. It was irritating and embarrassing, and the problem was getting worse.

We spent six weeks in Portland, renewing friendships and enjoying the hospitality of the Portland and Rose City yacht clubs. Chuck Schmiel generously lent us his pickup truck for our entire visit, which eliminated the eternal transportation problem that a cruiser faces.

We managed to get our boat jobs completed between dinners, dock parties, river excursions, and two slide presentations that we hosted.

A plastics company fabricated a state-of-the-art water tank to replace the cracked one. The very word "tank" still sent me into a cold sweat after the fuel tank episode. The water tank installation wasn't easy, but it was child's play compared to the fuel tank job, which by this time I had blown completely out of proportion.

After a few beers at one of the parties, I was lying on my back on the living room floor holding a footstool in the air, acting out the tank removal. I described the feat as "dwarfing all other forms of human endeavor" which Molly thought was a little much. In retrospect, I'm fairly certain she thought my entire act was a little much.

I had the fuel injectors rebuilt and spent one whole day

lying across the engine adjusting the timing of the high-pressure fuel pump. The net result of the expense and my labor was about a two-percent reduction in smoke. It would have to do for the moment. We were heading south, and it didn't matter if the engine smoked in the ocean.

Our plan was to stop at Brookings, Oregon, a small coastal town near the California border, then put in at a few ports in the Golden State en route to San Diego, our jumping off place for Mexico and points south.

Before departing for Mexico we planned to file our income taxes, and I had some final polishing to do on my book manuscript. I had intended to complete the work in Portland, but the parties got in the way. We needed to stop someplace where we didn't know anyone and be antisocial for a while.

On our way to Astoria we motored past the boathouse where we had lived and built *Swan* during the years 1973 to 1977. The aluminum boathouse with faded trim looked the same as we remembered it, but the surrounding area was a chockablock development of two-storied houseboats with town houses looming over them on the banks of the river. Living in a houseboat on the river had become the voguish thing to do. When we lived there in the early 1970's, it was the river-rattish thing to do.

Gale warnings were posted when we arrived at Astoria. The Coast Guard had closed the Columbia River Bar to small craft. It gave us a valid excuse to spend some time in Astoria engaged in some worthwhile pursuits such as drinking beer, eating smoked fish, and shooting pool with a great bunch of young sailors off a visiting U.S. Navy ship.

When the gale blew itself out, the sun broke through the overcast, which is a notable event on the Oregon coast. The year-round greenery and all of that excellent water comes with a price tag.

We took advantage of this meteorological phenomenon and sailed on the ebbing tide in the warm sunshine, reaching on the starboard tack in a light westerly.

The weather forecast promised three days of northerly winds at 15 to 20 knots, which was perfect for our run south along the coast. As predicted, the wind arrived in the late evening, driving us at good speed on a course parallel with the coastline, 30 miles offshore.

Sunrise on the third day revealed a northern sky full of black, menacing clouds. A sharply increased wind force belied the rosy forecast. The timing was bad. We had been closing with the coast on a course for Brookings that would take us within eight miles of Cape Blanco, a nasty point of land that was capable of kicking up mean seas in heavy weather.

If the wind held we could reach port by late afternoon at the speed we were making; however, I was beginning to have misgivings about the Brookings stop. I peered shoreward through binoculars, weighing the inherent risk of entering an unfamiliar harbor in heavy weather against the shelter and comfort one knows he will find there. The thought of a peaceful night's sleep was very appealing.

The north wind continued to build. Off Cape Blanco the Brookings question became moot. In a very short time we found ourselves sailing in large, alarmingly steep seas that were running at seven or eight-second intervals. I couldn't believe how fast the seas had built—Cape Blanco was doing its treacherous work.

Swan was bounding along on a beam reach under the jib alone; a point of sail that had suddenly become dangerous in these conditions, with the potential for a roll-down on the face of a breaking rogue wave.

That ominous thought scarcely had time to register when Molly shouted, "Watch out!" I turned just as a perfectly timed breaking sea crashed over the port quarter, inundating me with cold Pacific. *Swan* slued off before the rogue wave, heeling sharply and throwing me against the leeward coaming, giving my elbow a painful knock. The large drain emptied the partially flooded cockpit in a matter of seconds.

For a moment I lay sprawled on the cockpit seat, then I released the two slippery hitches on the lines that held the tiller in place and pushed it to windward. Molly held it there while I locked Vane in the neutral position. He had been struggling manfully to hold the course. Free from Vane's resistance, *Swan* fell off downwind.

I was astounded. Thirty minutes earlier we had been sailing in moderate seas, considering whether or not to enter a strange port, and now we were in danger of foundering.

Another monster sea made an unsuccessful attempt to come on board. *Swan* lifted in time in the quartering seas. She wasn't one bit happy about being pooped—it was an unwelcome and undignified first. I wasn't happy about it either. I had underestimated the effects of Cape Blanco.

Running off had been our long-standing procedure during storms when dealing with dangerous seas generated by adverse currents, or from the influence of capes such as Blanco, provided the wind direction in relation to the land permitted this course of action. No heroics—it's not a race—just keep the boatspeed down and get away from the threat.

We were plunging into the troughs far more quickly than my nervous system could tolerate. Soaked to the skin in the chilly wind, I made my way forward on the pitching deck to take down the jib while Molly held our downwind course.

There was, perhaps, a possibility that I harbored a trace of paranoia on the subject of running before the wind in steep-faced following seas. We had nearly lost it all in the Mozambique Channel in short-period, steep seas, and the memory of that fearful experience had not even begun to fade. The seas off Cape Blanco were by no means in a league with the ones we had encountered in the storm on the east coast of Africa. But enhanced by the steepness of their faces, and viewed through the gloomy mist in the evening twilight with eyes that were 10 years older, the menacing Cape Blanco seas were doing a passable imitation of their African counterparts. I didn't see my actions to decrease boatspeed as having anything to do with paranoia—I saw them as prudent and cautious. I hadn't heard of anyone dying of prudence and caution.

Pitchpoling was not a real concern. The seas were not large enough to inflict that ultimate catastrophe. Burying the bow after surfing down the face of a sea, sluing off into a broach, and being knocked down or rolled over was the more probable danger.

Swan's cutaway forefoot and spade rudder, which was positioned well aft, made her very suitable for running off in a deep seaway. Her fin keel was not likely to slice into a wave obliquely and skew her off during a rapid plunge into the trough. However, the proper boatspeed was critical to a controlled descent. Too slow a speed was nearly as bad as too fast. At slower speeds the loss of inertia and reduced steerageway make a boat vulnerable to being pummeled by an overtaking wave, creating the possibility of broaching.

From previous experience we had determined that five knots was the optimum speed for Swan to maintain when running off in heavy weather. We were making less than that under bare poles. I started the engine and increased our speed with a power assist to five knots.

I chose to use the engine rather than fly the storm jib because it was much easier to maintain a fixed speed under power. This also eliminated the problem of the sail being blanketed by the seas when the boat was deep in the trough, and it gave us the means to instantly power out of a broach. We were not sailing purists; especially in matters of safety.

With the engine ensuring a reasonably constant speed, I set Vane to steer a course that put the wind and seas one point on the starboard quarter. This appreciably reduced the angle of descent into the valleys between the seas, lessening the risk of the bow digging in. Our course was a few degrees divergent from the coast, which was soothing to my nerves with nightfall approaching.

To guard against the possibility of rounding up in a breaking rogue sea I trimmed the tiller to windward, slightly resisting the self-steering gear. This eliminated any slack in the system, because the main rudder, which was totally independent of the steering rudder, was perpetually trying to bring the boat back toward the dead downwind course.

In the midst of this elemental violence a group of dolphins romped robustly into the scene, reveling in the turbulent seas, and accentuating our feelings of being out of our element. For a dolphin, a gale off a rugged cape was the equivalent of an afternoon at Disneyland. They surfed down the faces of the waves, emitting gleeful squeaks like kids in a schoolyard. Their visits were always welcome—this one especially. There was little doubt that they wished *Swan* well.

I rigged a canvas windbreak between the backstays to block the spray that occasionally flew over the weathercloths, and huddled under it in my foul-weather gear with my feet inside one of the cockpit lockers that was warmed by the heat of the engine.

Night fell.

Molly supported the situation from below, keeping an eye on the depthsounder and monitoring CN's fixes. From time to time the main hatch would slide open a crack and a hand would appear holding a cup of coffee or soup. Are we having fun yet?

As we drew away from the cape the period of the waves lengthened. It was still blowing a gale, but the seas were no longer threatening. We raised the jib and carried on through the coal-black night.

Breaking our normal routine, I took the first watch. I settled into my sheltered corner of the cockpit armed with binoculars, a thermos of coffee, a handful of cookies, and a timer. It soon became apparent that my snug little spot was far too conducive to slumber. The lulling effect of the residual engine heat, the canvas windbreak that doubled as an all-too-comfortable headrest, and the knowledge that we were out of immediate danger had a seductive and somnolent effect on me.

This was no time for leadened eyelids and relaxed vigilance! A Force 8 gale was still blowing, the crashing surf was less than one hour away, visibility was two miles at best, we didn't have radar, and it was possible for us to close with northbound shipping at the rate of one mile every three minutes or faster.

I closed the heat-radiating hatch, swallowed two caffeine tablets from a bottle stored within reach in a rack inside the companionway, and sat erect in the cockpit drinking a steaming mug of coffee. The timer was set for 20 minutes and the depthsounder alarm would ring if we were set in to the 40 fathom curve. Should the depth alarm sound, it would bring Molly on deck in a flash.

The continental shelf shoals gradually along most of the west coast of the United States, which makes a depthsounder a valuable piece of navigation equipment. I crossed a bearing taken on a navigation light with the depthsounder reading, establishing an approximate position in the rough conditions as a backup to the electronic fixes.

Swan's chart table was equipped with two bright incandescent lights and a small red light on a gooseneck for checking headings and the like without destroying one's night vision. The red light was inadequate for plotting fixes, or tedious at best, because of the small area it illuminated.

I switched on the bright lights, partially retaining my night vision by using a trick that I had learned from a character whom I had met some years earlier at the Hawaii Yacht Club bar. He claimed that he had been a member of the CIA, and his stories about his shadowy past were entertaining, but highly dubious. They grew more entertaining and more dubious with each scotch and soda that he downed. (According to him, people in the spook trade in the western countries were partial to scotch and soda—it was an image thing.) He told me that he had been trained to instantly close one eye if a light was flashed on while he was engaged in some clandestine, nocturnal mission; because when the offending light was extinguished, the eye that had been closed retained its night vision.

The spook was right. It works. I used this technique many times to study the chart, or while using the head. (Warning: there is a depth perception drawback for males using this trick in the head.)

Assured that we were making off the land, and fully alert from the triple jolt of caffeine, I turned the steering duties completely over to Vane.

Running off had gotten us out of danger. It had become our natural response when we sensed ourselves getting into trouble, or when an unexpected problem arose. It buys time to think. Running off stabilizes the boat while a sail is taken down in a sudden squall, a loose halyard is retrieved, or while coping with a gear failure. It can be an effective means of dealing with an emergency, or avoiding a potentially dangerous situation.

Most sailors are conditioned to bring the bow into the wind to raise or lower the headsail. With some, it may date back to their dinghy sailing days, or when they sailed larger boats in confined waters, or from their racing experience. It made sense in those situations. It was the correct thing to do. But the tactics change somewhat on a shorthanded cruising sailboat in the open ocean. To bring the bow into the wind often means heading into large seas and dealing with the problem of maintaining the boat's position while the foredeck work is completed. The simple solution in heavy weather is to run off.

In the early days of our cruising experience we braved the perils of the foredeck while bashing into head seas, rather than sacrifice the loss of distance caused by running off, or even falling off a point or two. Gradually we came to realize that no place on the planet was so wonderful that it couldn't wait a little longer while we ran off during heavy weather to work the foredeck in a safe and civilized manner.

There is a vast difference between dousing a headsail in the lee of the main on a relatively stable deck while running off, and taking it down with salt spray blasting in your face and green water sheeting over the heaving foredeck.

On the afternoon of the following day we approached the inviting, though intimidating arms of the breakwaters at Eureka, California on Humboldt Bay. Great combers crashed with awesome power on the windward jetty as *Swan* motorsailed through the entrance of this welcome sanctuary.

We powered slowly against the ebbing tide past the harbor-bound tuna boats rafted two or three deep at the wharves lining the channel. Twelve years had passed since we had stopped here. Nothing was as we remembered it.

Just as I was considering dropping the hook at the edge of the channel, Molly spotted a cluster of masts in the distance. We motored toward them and discovered that a much-needed, large marina had been built on what had been a sandspit on our earlier visit to Eureka.

To our dismay, boats were rafted two abreast at the fuel dock. There appeared to be a vacant berth next to a fishing trawler where a party was in full swing. The tide was running out at a fast clip. This, coupled with the strong crosswind and the jam-packed marina had more than enough ingredients for a Chinese fire drill. Docking *Swan* in conditions such as these had never been our long suit; a deficiency now magnified by the unreliable, rapidly deteriorating engine which seemed to be on the verge of entering the final throes of death.

I gambled on a run at the berth adjacent to the party boat. We motored along the row of trawlers, holding *Swan's* bow fully 20 degrees to starboard into the running tide to maintain the course. At the entrance to the slip I put the helm hard to port and gave the enfeebled diesel full throttle for a few seconds of turning thrust against the rudder, then shifted to reverse and revved the engine again, stopping the forward motion. I repeated the sequence and *Swan* pivoted quickly in a sharp right turn without overrunning the slip while being set smartly toward the downstream dock. When the turn was complete, we powered straight against the current into the slip. The crosswind set us gently against the finger pier as I held the position in forward gear. Molly stepped nonchalantly onto the dock and cleated off the bow line.

Our festive audience on the party boat didn't see the sidelong glance of relief the mate gave me. However, they could not help but notice the large albacore that we had caught earlier in the day. It was lying prominently on the deck expressly for their benefit.

It was a wonder they could see anything. *Swan's* overworked, overheated engine had laid down a black smoke screen that would have gladdened the heart of a World War II naval commander running the North Atlantic U-Boat gauntlet. But commercial fisherman are not easily perturbed—except about matters pertaining to the Japanese long-line fishing fleet—and they held out two beers to us as a welcome.

During the three days that we were holed up in port waiting for a favorable weather window, we were willingly led astray by this raucous and convivial group of fishermen. At one rowdy session in the marina bar we were requested by the manager to keep the noise down. He said we were disturbing the patrons in the adjacent dining room. I had been telling the tuna men some sea stories which they found humorous. After the second or third warning, one particularly loud outburst of laughter was the final straw. The manager showed every manjack of us the door (including Molly). The party moved to one of the trawlers where the incredulous fishermen accused me of getting them "eighty-sixed" out of their own bar!

Molly added glazed barbecued tuna to her recipe collection during this stop. It was a specialty of one of the fishermen. Beer *must* be served with this dish, which is probably why it was so popular with the tuna men.

I committed the recipe to memory at an intemperate gathering on a trawler in the small hours of the morning somewhere between an off-key rendition of "The Sloop John B." and a robust rendering of "Lucille."

Resisting Molly's urging that I lay down my "precious ukulele" for a moment and jot down the recipe, I assured her that I would relate it to her verbatim later—not to worry.

Two days later, reaching southward in a light westerly, the mate stood poised over me with pencil and pad in hand as I lay dozing on the settee.

"The recipe," she said succinctly.

"The recipe?" I said. "What recipe?"

"Glazed barbecued tuna," she said in clipped words as she flipped the cover of the pad over like "Ms. Steno of the Year."

In the seafood section of Molly's cookbook the following recipe can be found for glazed barbecued tuna, transcribed—scrupulously—word for word as I dictated it from the settee:

—about 1 part soy sauce
—roughly 2 parts honey
—1 or 2 parts butter
—some slivers of garlic
—salt and pepper too—I think—no, just pepper

—put the stuff in a pan and cook it for a while until it
looks like it's blended together
—paint it on the fish as it cooks on the barbecue and let it
get burned a little
—it serves as many people as you made enough for

A pertinent note from Molly:

> This is a very forgiving recipe. Exact quantities of
> the ingredients are not critical to the dish (fortu-
> nately). I should add that it is much better if "they"
> do not involve themselves with things of this na-
> ture

It was September 1989. We had time to kill—about four
months. We did not want to sail for Mexico until we had filed
our income taxes, and a short stay in Southern California
would give me time to complete the final work on my book
manuscript. Also, it was becoming increasingly clear that the
engine was in much worse condition than I had originally
thought. It would require major work.

Oxnard, California was our immediate destination. Molly's
uncle lived there, and he had checked the availability of moorage facilities in the area. There were several short-term slips for
rent at fairly reasonable rates. As it turned out, stopping at Oxnard was one of our better decisions.

Five hundred miles of coast-hopping, ship-dodging, and fog-
bound sailing in the slow lane later, *Swan* was moored in a marina in Oxnard with her waterline covered with Santa Barbara
Channel crude oil.

Much of the passage had been a strain. The normal anxi-
eties associated with motoring through long stretches of fog
without benefit of radar were augmented by concerns about
red-line engine temperatures and precipitous drops in oil pressure. One night stands out sharply in my mind.

Swan lay nearly motionless, 15 miles offshore near San
Francisco in thick, zero-visibility fog. I had shut down the overheated engine, which was on the verge of seizing. Without a

breath of wind stirring, or an erg of reliable power to drive *Swan*, I was thankful for the fair distance we were from shore. Heavy ship traffic was our chief concern.

Determined to find the cause of the overheating problem, I dismantled as much of the cooling system as possible. I was lying on the cabin sole replacing the raw water pump impeller when I heard a distant Whumpa! Whumpa! Whumpa! reverberating through the hull. A ship's propeller!

I placed my ear against the cold, clammy floorboards and listened again. The sound transmission through the still water was remarkably clear. The ship was close and getting closer!

A classic scene from submarine movies that I had seen over the years flashed through my mind: the young intense sailor wearing the sonar earphones; the destroyer bearing down on the vulnerable submarine, black smoke billowing from her funnels, while the sub's crew frantically prepared to dive—only *Swan* couldn't do that!

Whumpa! Whumpa! Whumpa!

Now Molly heard it and was calling to me from the cockpit. Her words were lost as a booming blast of a ship's horn rent the thick night air. Impotent, in a word, described our situation.

The horn blew again. It seemed to have moved to our right as we faced the general direction of the sound. Three more times, at about one-minute intervals, the horn blew, moving ever farther to our right. The moving sound impression was so distinct that we could easily imagine the black mass of a ship passing, perhaps two or three hundred yards to seaward. Then the horn fell silent, and the thumping of the propeller faded into the night.

It was fairly obvious that the lookout on the bridge of the passing ship had seen us on radar and had responsibly sounded his horn.

The experience was nerve-wracking, but also reassuring. From previous testing of the effectiveness of our radar reflector, we knew that it returned a sharp signal up to eight miles distant in medium seas when sea return (clutter) was not a significant factor. Of necessity, ships' radar screens are closely monitored in heavy fog. This, I believe, makes running slowly or lying-to in open waters less hazardous for a small craft than it seems, if the boat is equipped with a properly mounted and tested radar reflector. Colliding with a fishing trawler running on autopilot with no one on watch, or with some other small vessel, is probably a more realistic danger in foggy conditions.

But having done the majority of our cruising in the tropics where fog is not a problem, I was not at all sure of the validity of my conjecture. Nor was the mate, who was standing in the stern peering into the murky gloom in the direction of the disappearing ghost ship.

6

MOLLY FOUND A JOB in less than a week at a Naval Air Station, working in the medical field. This made the purchase of a vehicle an immediate priority. Her uncle lent us his car which made the problem of finding wheels less of an ordeal than it might have been.

After three frustrating days of kicking tires we found a cruiser's special—a throwaway car. It was a sickly green, four-door something or other that became known around the marina as the Green Machine. The odometer had flipped over at least once, and sported some youthful digits, but the prodigious quantities of motor oil that the engine consumed told the real story. The car had a capacious pre-oil crunch carcass and a cavernous trunk, and it soon became a mobile warehouse as we shopped the food sales, stocking up for our impending south-of-the-border adventure.

The Green Machine suffered only one small breakdown during the four months that we owned the car. It served the purpose, and we managed to ignore the knocks in the engine and the growling gears as we piloted the ponderous hulk over the sunny roads of Southern California.

Like a surgeon studying the ravages of some horrible disease, I stood staring down at the innards of the diesel engine. The cylinders were worn into ovals; the pistons fairly rattled about, and the valves and valve seats were badly burned. I never even bothered to look at the connecting rods and bearings. I knew. The insidious effects of the intrusion of salt water and 13 years of rough service had taken a severe toll on the engine. It would be a mistake to throw money away on an old worn-out diesel. I had a feeling our bank account was about to suffer a substantial hit.

A savage blow was closer to the mark. By the time it was over the tally was well above $7000, and I did all of the work myself.

In California you don't replace an engine, you "repower." To repower, you go to a repowering center. If you haven't already guessed, repowering costs more than just replacing the engine. It's like buying a used car at a lot that sells "pre-owned" cars. Pre-owned cars cost more than used cars.

To be honest, the hefty bill was a lot of my doing. I never know when to stop. I become almost possessed when I launch into a project. All traces of the old engine had to be removed. The new engine had to appear as if it had been conceived in *Swan's* womb. I lined the walls of the engine compartment with aluminum sheeting to cover the places where the old wires, cables, and hoses had been attached. New fuel lines, new wiring, new motor mounts, new hoses, new everything was installed along with the 25-horsepower, three-cylinder, Universal diesel engine.

The new engine's rotation was the opposite of the old one, requiring the purchase of a propeller. I bought a new three-blade prop and a pre-owned one for a spare.

To complete *Swan's* mechanical rebirth, I replaced the original refrigeration compressor, which was still functioning perfectly, in direct violation of the rule: "If it ain't broke don't fix it."

In addition to the factory-suggested engine spare parts kit, I ordered several more engine components that I thought should be on board. To be certain that the parts were the correct ones, I installed them where practicable and stored the original parts.

I stopped short of installing the seawater pump impeller. This proved to be a mistake. The factory shipped the wrong impeller, and I used the incorrect part number to purchase three more.

Months later, in Mexico, I discovered the error while assisting another cruiser repair his engine, which happened to be the same model as *Swan*'s diesel. I managed to arrange for the correct impellers to be shipped to us with assistance from a fellow cruiser who was returning to California. Six weeks later the parts arrived via an undetermined overland carrier, a cruising trimaran, and finally another cruising boat that sailed into the anchorage in a small port in the northern part of the Baja Peninsula with its VHF radio crackling: "*Swan Swan Swan*—we've got your parts."

Before leaving on an extended cruise, make arrangements with a reliable, full-range chandlery to handle the procurement and shipping of parts and equipment. There are chandleries that specialize in this type of service. They are set up to be reached by single sideband radio, fax, letter, or telephone. The usual and simplest method of payment for services rendered is to leave a credit card number on file with the chandlery before departing. Preferably your own.

When the engine and mechanical systems had been thoroughly tested, I began the intimidating task of refurbishing the complete interior of the boat. I created a horrendous mess each day, and managed to get it at least partially cleaned up before the Green Machine clunked into the parking lot in the evening.

In January we hauled the boat out of the water and applied two coats of anti-fouling paint on the bottom; waxed the topsides, and polished everything that was supposed to shine. *Swan* sparkled on the inside and outside—a perennial debutante—ready to sail the pristine waters of the Sea of Cortez.

At last I had some time to work on my book. For six hours each day for two weeks I sat before a portable word processor and polished the work until I was satisfied that it was as professional as I could make it.

The editor of Sheridan House Inc., a publishing company in New York, had expressed an interest in reading the manuscript. On the day before we sailed south I mailed it to him—sort of a writer's version of a Hail Mary Pass.

Our original intention was to provision the boat in San Diego, but having the luxury of an automobile had altered our plans. Most of the shopping had been completed, and the Green Machine was down on her lines.

We spent an entire day coursing through the aisles of supermarkets and discount stores, checking off the final items on Molly's list.

Before we packed away the staggering array of food, soap, paper products, and bags full of sundry items that filled the cockpit, we emptied the lockers and thoroughly cleaned them. We vacuumed under the indoor/outdoor carpeting that lined the lockers and prevented condensation from forming on the hull. Liberal quantities of a cockroach killing powder was then sprinkled into all the nooks and crannies where cockroaches hide, and under the hull liner.

The active ingredient in the powder is boric acid. Read the label. It should be almost pure boric acid. The product can be found in the pest control section of department stores and supermarkets under various brand names. It is the answer to roach control. It works, and will continue to work even if it becomes caked from humidity.

The powder is easier to find in southern states where cockroaches are prevalent. If the powder cannot be found in the variety store in Kodiak, Alaska, whence you are sailing nonstop to Borneo, buy medicinal boric acid at the Kodiak Pharmacy. It will be more expensive, but it will work.

Avoid bringing cardboard boxes on board unless you are absolutely sure they are fresh and clean. Roaches will lay their eggs under the flaps, or in the corrugation of the cardboard, and the newborn roaches will live on the glue until word reaches them about the good stuff in the galley.

Leafy vegetables, bunches of bananas, and other produce where roaches and a variety of pests could be hiding were routinely immersed in the sea in a net bag before they were brought on board *Swan*, then rinsed in fresh water. If the harbor was polluted, the fruit and vegetables were washed or immersed in a bucket of fresh water at the dock. On more than one occasion I have seen a roach or spider pop to the surface and indignantly swim away from such ungracious hosts.

Port Louis, Mauritius had the finest open market of any that we had seen; it also had a huge population of rats that roamed the streets in broad daylight. There wasn't much question as to where they ate their nightly meals. In places like this we added a dollop of bleach to a bucket of water to kill any disease-causing microorganisms. Supposedly, the bleach has a preserving effect if it is allowed to air dry on the fruit and vegetables.

Suddenly turning on a light at night to be greeted by the sight of the galley counter alive with cockroaches does not have to be part of the cruising experience. If you see two or three roaches, you've probably got a hundred. The best time to launch an attack on cockroaches is *before* they get on board.

The problem of cockroaches on board vessels is not exactly new. It is my understanding that some pertinent words were spoken about the subject by Noah, one of the first cruising sailors. Unfortunately, his words were not recorded in Genesis; probably because his thoughts on cockroaches would hardly have been considered newsworthy in the midst of a flood that was 15 cubits higher than Mt. Everest.

As the story goes, sometime in the middle of his epic voyage, he was seen standing on the quarterdeck of the ark roaring at his crew: "What do you mean they're everywhere? I only brought two roaches on board."

We had learned a lesson about provisioning from our earlier voyage. *Swan* had sailed to the South Pacific stocked with large quantities of basic, nutritional foods. We had been so preoccupied with food that was "good for us" that we neglected to store an adequate supply of our favorite things to eat.

During the circumnavigation we thoroughly enjoyed sampling the cuisine of the countries and island republics that we visited. For example, we became very fond of Indonesian curry, deep fried breadfruit chips, and South African meat pies. However, these new dining experiences in no way diminished our love of Mexican food. By the time we had reached Tonga, we had depleted most of our meager supply of the necessary ingredients to prepare Mexican meals. There wasn't one tortilla left in the freezer. And you just try to find a corn tortilla in the Kingdom of Tonga.

Our attempt at making tortillas while anchored inside the Great Astrolabe Reef in Fiji was one of our more notable culinary disasters. Even the school of scavenger fish that were hanging around the boat, fighting over every morsel of discarded food, headed for the nearest reef when they saw the great globs of congealed cornmeal plummeting to the bottom like cannon balls.

This time, we concentrated on a balance of provisions, and if we erred, it was on the side of storing too much of our favorite foods. Given our immediate cruising destination, we went light on tortillas and tequila, and heavy on pasta, soy sauce, mayonnaise, popcorn, artificial sweeteners, alfalfa seeds for sprouts, saltine crackers, and anything that we normally used or consumed which we thought would be difficult to find in Mexico and Central America.

High on our list of provisioning priorities were instant ramen noodles. The noodles are quick and easy to prepare, and are especially soothing if one is experiencing butterflies in the stomach on a rough passage. They were packaged 24 to a carton that measured a compact 4"x10"x16". We bought three cases and risked the roaches, keeping the noodles packed in the cartons.

Small bugs will appear in double- and even triple-packaged spaghetti and other dry foods after prolonged storage in the tropics. We could never find any evidence that the bugs invaded the packages. Apparently they were always there as spores or something of that nature. How they are able to flourish in powdery dry food is a wonderment, but they do.

The problem can be minimized by storing the dry food against the hull where it will maintain the approximate temperature of the ocean, which is usually cooler than the general interior of the boat in the tropics. Whenever possible, buy recently processed food from air-conditioned supermarkets that have a fast inventory turnover.

Many food products have toll-free telephone numbers written on the package, encouraging the customer to call for product information. We did this often, and found the customer relations people very helpful in deciphering the coded processing or expiration date and other pertinent data.

We dated all packaged and canned foods with a permanent marker felt pen, and used the oldest food first without fail.

Regardless of precautions, bugs will still be found in some of the dry foods. The best approach to the problem is not to worry about it until the product is used. The offending critters can be washed down the sink drain.

Having dealt with roaches and food bugs, I will spend a moment on book bugs; tiny busy bugs that are often found in older books, particularly in the tropics. Their taste in literature knows no bounds. They will digest a dime-store novel, and then wade into a few pages of Homer without missing a beat.

Whenever we traded books, the new additions to *Swan*'s library were routinely put in a plastic bag and placed at the bottom of the freezer for 24 hours. This finished off any unwelcome guests.

Moisture is the eternal enemy of a yacht. During humid weather, dampness permeates the boat, causing drawers to stick, mildew to form, and charts to curl. It makes life generally sticky and uncomfortable. The damp, salt air can be devastating to moisture-vulnerable items that are carelessly stored.

Our solution to preventing rust, mildew, and other moisture-caused problems was careful packaging and the use of silica gel, a moisture absorbing agent that we obtained from a chemical supply company. The name is misleading. It is not a gel per se, but a porous drier in small rock-like granule form.

When Molly said good-bye to the nine-to-five world, we saved her old nylon stockings. The nylons were cut into short lengths and knotted at one end, forming a small bag. The bag was filled with silica gel and the open end was tied in a loose knot, creating a sphere about the size of a golf ball. These pouches of thirsty silica were placed in the airtight containers and pressure-sealed plastic bags in which engine parts, electronic components, and other moisture-sensitive equipment were stored.

The type we used was color-indicating, which means that it turns from blue to light pink when saturated. It's a simple matter to dehydrate the material by heating it in a pan at a very low heat until the blue color returns. It can be used indefinitely.

One last point about damage-control. Clothing stored in hanging lockers should be hung on plastic or wooden hangers; never on hangers made of steel or any other metal that can corrode and ruin the garments. The clothing should be prevented from swinging with the motion of the boat by means of shock-cord ties or some other device. It doesn't require much time for a hanger to wear through your favorite shoreside outfit if it's allowed to rub unrestricted against the locker bulkhead.

One of the few advantages of owning a throwaway car is that if any part of the purchase price is recouped, it's like a gift. So we felt fortunate when we sold the Green Machine for about half of what we paid for it in a cash-on-the-hood deal in the marina parking lot.

On the morning after a great bon-voyage party that was thrown for us by our friends at the marina, "the B Dock gang," *Swan's* spanking new engine powered us through the breakwater at Oxnard, sans smoke.

We motored south toward Santa Catalina Island in a flat calm. Molly was spared my usual grumbling about the absence of wind, because our plan was to power or motorsail the entire 135 miles to San Diego to shake down the new engine.

Near midnight, a cold front moving down from Alaska caught up with us as we were passing north of Catalina Island, bringing heavy rain. The sharply reduced visibility made crossing the parallel shipping lanes leading in and out of Los Angeles an exercise in cautious navigation.

The running lights of the outbound ships, tugs, and sundry craft were obscured against the blazing panorama of city lights. My eyeglasses were rendered useless in the driving rain, so I turned the piloting duties over to Molly, who has excellent distance vision. I rigged the sailing awning to shelter us from the deluge, and retreated to the galley where I whipped up a kettle of ramen noodles.

The trip to San Diego was a damp, dismal stretch of motoring, made tolerable by the knowledge that with every hour that passed we were five miles farther south.

A more immediate source of comfort was the cockpit heater I had devised during the engine replacement work.

I installed a 4" diameter plastic access port with a sealing cover on the forward face of the cockpit, directly above the engine. A 12-volt fan was positioned inside the engine compartment to blow through the port. The fan was actuated by the ignition switch, and could be overridden by a switch on the fan itself. Flexible clothes-dryer exhaust duct can be used to conduct the engine heat to the cockpit area if the engine is not directly beneath the cockpit.

The combination of the awning and the engine heat swirling around our legs gave a needed boost to our spirits as we threaded our way through the kelp beds in the approaches to San Diego.

We stayed as guests of the San Diego Yacht Club, and life was a lark. The pleasant and plush environment there helped assuage our sense of frustration created by our efforts to satisfy the numerous requirements of the Mexican Consulate for a visa and cruising permit. The Mexican bureaucracy has developed paperwork to a fine art: visas for each of us; crew lists written in Spanish and submitted in quadruplicate; an import permit for *Swan*; a fishing license for Molly and me, and for *Swan*, and for the dinghy!

After three bus trips across town our papers were in order, and we were finally set for the passage south to Margaritaville.

7

TWO DAYS OUT, 130 miles south of San Diego, *Swan* sat dead in the water, waiting for the wind.

Log entry, March 9, 1990: "Wind fell seriously ill at 2030—succumbed at 2115—buried at 2200."

Wind or no wind, it didn't matter. We were finally on our way! Nine months into the voyage and there wasn't a foreign stamp in our passports. That would soon change. Our taxes were filed, our business ties were severed, and *Swan* was in fine fettle. Dropping out of society for a while had a marvelous appeal.

On the eve of this passage a vague uneasiness had crept over us; not unlike the feeling one experiences the first time that the children are left home alone. The last time Molly and I had sailed into the sunset, leaving the country to shift for itself, it had gone to hell in a handbasket.

We had locked a portion of our savings into long-term investments, then watched interest rates shoot through the ozone hole during President Carter's watch. The dollar had plummeted so low that we could scarcely bring ourselves to approach the foreign money exchange window at the bank. The abysmal exchange rate did, however, broaden our itinerary, as we were drawn toward some very remote islands where word of our debased currency had not reached the natives, and we could still buy coconuts six for a dollar.

The less than dazzling performance of our investments during the first voyage was a painful subject that I assiduously avoided; mainly because I had been the mastermind behind the financial strategy. I assured Molly that this time it would be different—very different. I had formulated an investment plan that was in tune with the times. Her fixed stare told me that I had been wise not to describe the plan as "foolproof" as I nearly did.

In the 1988 general election we went to the polling place in Waikiki and voted for every Republican in sight. I lost sleep staying up to watch the late news, just to read George Bush's lips one more time. The words were music to my ears: reinstate the capital gains tax law; no new taxes; expand the job base; the budget deficit was headed south; and the dollar would once again be strong.

Perfect! The scenario was obvious to anyone with a grain of sense. The economy would overheat and interest rates would rise to cool it off. Probably double digits! I wasn't about to lock in our investments, long-term, at some paltry 8 or 9 percent. Short-term was the play. Let them rise with the financial tide!

In 1981 we had returned to the United States looking for employment and found the country in the midst of a recession. But the '90s would be a whole new ball game. George's steady hand was on the helm of the Ship of State. I was ebullient. Don't worry honey, there will be Jobs! Jobs! Jobs!

I knew, of course, that it was patently absurd to think that our leaving the country could have any possible bearing whatsoever on the economy. Our earlier experience had been a coincidence, pure and simple. To believe otherwise would be nothing less than superstitious nonsense. But just to play it safe, we slipped *Swan*'s mooring lines before dawn in San Diego and sneaked out of the country.

When the wind finally came, it was from the west-northwest, and it built steadily during the afternoon. With the fresh breeze just forward of the quarter, *Swan* made a comfortable six knots flying the reacher and storm trysail.

Because it was getting late in the cruising season in Mexico, we had decided to sail nonstop to Cabo San Lucas at the southern tip of the Baja California peninsula. From there we planned to meander north into the Sea of Cortez, where we would spend the hurricane season (See Fig. 7).

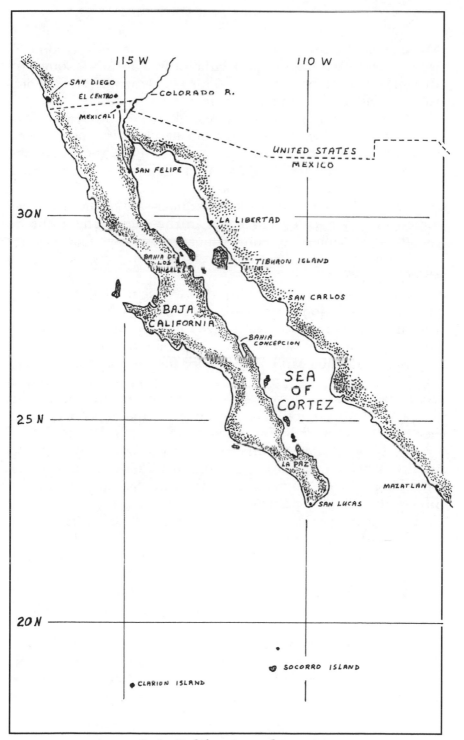

FIG. 7 *Baja California and Sea of Cortez*

Our sailing course was laid out to intersect a waypoint 50 miles west of Isla Cedros, an island located a short distance off the coast at 28° North latitude. This course would take us outside the bulk of the shipping traffic.

In the evening the wind increased enough that we took in the reacher and hanked on the working jib in its place. About 0200, on my watch, the ride got rougher. I furled the trysail and we ran with only the jib. This eased the motion considerably, but we were under-sailing the boat.

At sunrise we were no longer under-sailing the boat—we were flying! We sailed 275 miles in the succeeding 48 hours under the jib alone in a Force 6 nor'wester in perfect weather conditions: 80 degrees without a cloud in the sky. No fog, no ships, no worries.

During this romp to the south we caught a fat albacore. In the rough conditions, we didn't realize that a fish had hit the trolling line. We must have dragged it a fair distance, because the fish seemed almost anxious to come aboard for dinner.

Molly poached part of the fish for the evening meal, deviating slightly from her "any and all" fish recipe as she is wont to do. During these creative sessions in the galley, the mate often speaks rhetorically (talks to herself). On this occasion I heard her say, "How do you know when yogurt goes bad?"

At 24°N we altered course to close with Cabo San Lucas. The northwest wind had faded to a civilized 12 knots; perfect for approaching the land. To make amends for my lackadaisical navigation effort during the passage, I took a round of evening star sights, which fixed our position 60 miles northwest of the headland.

I cannot recall another night of sailing that equalled the perfection of this starlit night. Using the heavens as a compass, I spent my watch on the foredeck lying on cushions, propped against the forward slope of the cabin. Overhead, a satellite made its lonely transit across the sky against a spectacular celestial backdrop.

I lay there contemplating the odds against my being there, lying on the deck of an ocean sailing yacht in the Pacific Ocean. Someone who grew up in Indiana and never set foot on a sailboat until he was 36, nor had the slightest idea how to sail

92

one. Then to find a mate with the same "vast" experience who was receptive to my notion that we build a boat, quit our jobs, and sail to the South Pacific. Then to end up circumnavigating the earth. Big odds against something like that happening—like winning a lottery. But I *was* there, and I was still as excited about our next adventure as in the beginning.

The balmy breeze filled the reacher, driving *Swan* at four knots through long, overtaking rollers. At this speed there was no possibility of reaching land before dawn, which enhanced my feeling of well-being on this perfect tropical night.

To round out this idyllic sail, a small group of dolphins paid *Swan* a visit; but they soon tired of such a leisurely pace and continued on their way.

The breeze freshened at sunrise as we approached the cape. With such a favorable wind driving the boat, we opted to by-pass San Lucas, hoping to reach Bahia Los Frailes, an anchorage on the eastern side of the peninsula, before nightfall. It would be a race against the sun.

With Cabo San Lucas astern, we changed course to east-northeast, putting the brisk wind on the port beam. We hoisted the main and steered manually under a full press of sail, covering 23 miles in three hours. Vane had steered every inch of the way from San Diego, and he was undoubtedly miffed about being relieved when the heavy canvas was flying.

The fair wind that had driven us so easily into the Sea of Cortez, now became unfavorable as our course bore off to the northward. Despite *Swan*'s gallant effort, it was apparent that nightfall would win the race to the anchorage. We were not going to begin our cruise in Mexican waters by attempting to anchor in an unfamiliar place in failing light. I brought the bow through the wind, backwinding the jib. Molly eased out the reefed main and I put the helm down. *Swan* crabbed off the land, hove-to, forereaching slowly into the open sea.

An easy night of short naps passed, with an alarm clock set at 45-minute intervals. CN punched out an updated position about once each hour, which was reassuring input on this windy, dark night.

The dawn brought no change in the adverse wind. Flying

our trusty twosome, the jib and storm trysail, we spent the day making up to weather along the barren coast. The sun was well below the mountains when the anchor chain rattled over the bow rollers in a small cove called Los Muertos. The CQR anchor bit into Mexican sand for the first time; nine days and 910 passage miles from San Diego.

Rejuvenated by 10 straight hours of rest, I was at the helm, motoring at first light along the coast toward La Paz while Molly prepared fish tacos for breakfast. The mate isn't shackled by the bonds of orthodoxy.

The Mexican officials at La Paz were helpful and courteous during the confusing port-clearance routine. This came as a pleasant surprise after the tales to the contrary that we had heard. During our eight-month stay in Mexico we observed many problems between cruisers and Mexican officials. With rare exceptions, they were brought on by the cruisers.

Although we were often put off by the stacks of paperwork and make-work redundancy, it was their country and we played by their rules. As a consequence we had no problems with officials during the time we were there. An attempt to speak Spanish, no matter how poor an attempt, is very well-received in Mexico. We found that a few polite words in the local language were appreciated in most of the foreign countries we visited.

The anchorage in front of Marina de La Paz was jam-packed with cruising boats. The marina is the hub of the cruising community in La Paz. We had arrived just in time to participate in Race Week. Informal races among the cruising boats are held at a nearby island, Caleta Partida, and are really an excuse for a week-long bash.

We planned to attend, as a short vacation would be relaxing before we faced the six-month grind of fishing, diving, sailing, and exploring the Sea of Cortez.

Approximately 120 boats, mainly from California, were anchored in the bay. It was the grand finale of the winter season before the cruisers returned home to go back to . . . to the "W" word.

There were scheduled activities on the beach every day and parties on the yachts that ran far into the night. While Molly was trying to corrupt the judges who would be passing judgement on her "authentic Hawaiian Chili" in the chili cook-off, I attended the bikini contest and an impromptu wet T-shirt competition. Because of my nearsightedness, I crowded my way to the front of the raucous crowd where I could further my study of the female form; a discipline that has held my interest since I was about six, when I first developed an interest in art.

Several outrageously good guitar and banjo players were present at a cockpit wingding on board *Shirley L*, a sailboat owned by Bill and Shirley Anderson and guarded by their faithful dog Margarita. I was intimidated by the musical talent around me and was reluctant to play my ukulele. My learning curve with the uke had gotten stuck on a plateau a few weeks after I began playing, 15 years before. As the margarita jug emptied, I sensed by the frequency of lyrical goof-ups that the musicians might have become less tone conscious. This assumption and the tequila emboldened me enough to strum a few chords. Frowns formed instantly on the players' faces when they realized that all of their instruments were out of tune.

At week's end, the great majority of the yachts sailed back to La Paz, homeward bound. *Swan* and a small group of yachts began a migration into the northern reaches of the Sea of Cortez, where, in splendid isolation, we would spend the hurricane season.

After the hyperactivity of Race Week it was pleasant to poke along, anchoring in secluded coves, snorkeling and fishing on the reefs. Our ultimate destination was Bahía de Los Angeles, a remote village 360 miles northwest of La Paz. Most of the basic necessities of daily living were available there, if one's needs were not too sophisticated. We planned to make the village our base during the hurricane season.

In the unlikely event that a tropical cyclone reached that far north, there is an inlet called Don Juan, about six miles from the village, where one can find refuge (See Fig. 8). There is no swell in this hurricane hole, which is nearly surrounded by land with a small opening to the sea. In time, it became the anchorage of choice for most of the boats. We returned there often, enjoying the camaraderie and pioneer-like interdependence that developed among the crews of the handful of yachts rattling around in the northern part of the sea.

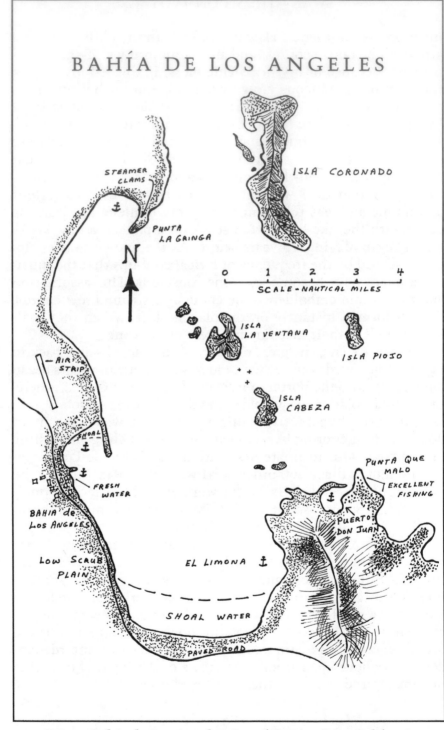

FIG. 8   *Bahía de Los Angeles, Sea of Cortez, Baja California*

It was at Bahía Concepción, en route north, that we were introduced to the incredible abundance of sea life in the Sea of Cortez. A few boats were anchored at Santispac, one of the many bays within Concepción. We had become briefly acquainted with the crews of some of the yachts during Race Week, but it is the way of cruising that formalities rarely get in the way, and a diving excursion to a nearby reef was planned almost immediately.

We were amazed by the large number of clams, pin scallops, and conch lying exposed on the sand in shallow water for the taking. Near the edge of the reef, in deeper water, bay scallops were in abundance—a real delicacy.,

The bay scallop is a fairly small mollusk of the type that was the model for the Shell gasoline sign, and when disturbed, it propels itself over the bottom by chattering like wind-up false teeth. We filled two large buckets with shellfish.

The community seafood feast took place on a large powerboat, a Grand Banks gold-plater that was owned by a very likable couple from California, Tom and Judy Smith. They had recently sold their business, and were enjoying the fruits of the American Dream at a relatively young age. I, of course, was aloof from such worldliness, even as I reached for another goblet of fine cognac, a tad of capers, and chilled ceviche, while lounging in the spacious luxury of the main saloon, as the sun set over the mountain range.

We had scarcely gotten ashore at Bahía de Los Angeles, when Molly learned that a small clinic that had been closed for a year for want of a doctor was reopening. A young doctor who was serving his 11-month social service period had just arrived from the mainland. His first patient was a pregnant woman who was imminently due to deliver. That was just too much for Molly, who had spent four years in the baby business in Labor and Delivery at Tripler Army Hospital in Honolulu. She volunteered her services, which were readily accepted by the nervous medical man facing his first maternity case.

Molly took one look at the examination room and returned to *Swan* for cleaning supplies. The smell of bleach permeated the clinic until she was satisfied that the environment was squeaky clean and the instruments were sterile. Her volunteer work at the clinic did not go unnoticed by the people of the village, and this accelerated our assimilation into the community.

The arrival of the vegetable truck was the main attraction each week at the village. It arrived every Saturday afternoon from some mysterious place, except when it didn't. When this calamity occurred the clerk in the little store would assure us that the truck would arrive mañana. We were soon to learn that mañana did not actually mean tomorrow. It meant that whatever was supposed to happen would, in all probability, happen sometime in the future—maybe.

The small fleet's dilemma was then whether to stay the night in the rolly anchorage in front of the village, or sail the six miles back to Don Juan, and return mañana for the next roll of the dice.

Solving this sticky problem usually required the consumption of a few beers under the shade of a palapa in front of Guermo's watering hole. Those who elected to sail back had to endure VHF radio transmissions from one of the powerboats in the fleet: "Why are your sails up? Is there something wrong with your engine?"

Most of the boats would stay the night with high hopes for mañana. As the evening breeze wafted in from the sea, we would idly wish that we had a copy of the Wall Street Journal to see how our paltry investments were doing in the face of the negative economic news that filtered down from the United States. We consoled each other that even though the young marrieds would have a bloody terrible time of it, which was a dirty shame, and the resulting inflation might place a strain on the country's pocketbook, interest rates would *surely* be going up soon.

Swan sailing in the
Sea of Cortez.

Interior of *Swan*—looking
forward.

Molly looking for
Cabo San Lucas—"Maybe
we waited too long to
turn left."

Dolphin guiding the way—Mexico to Panama passage.

Fifty-seven inch dorado—died of martinis.

Steamer clams gathered at Punta La Gringa, Bahía de Los Angeles.

Trigger fish caught in the Sea of Cortez.

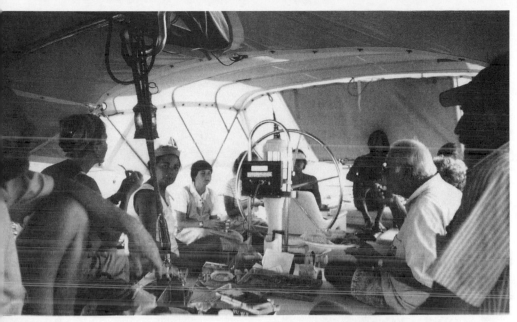

Molly's birthday party aboard *Danzante* at Don Juan.

Author mending sail—Mexico to Panama passage.

Marine boarding party at La Libertad, Mexico—One-eyed, four-legged "narc" in foreground.

A gathering of conspiratorial pelicans at Dog Bay, Sea of Cortez.

Locking down to Atlantic through Gatun Locks—Panama Canal.

The "Gaudy" Boat.

Swan sailing in the Gulf of Panama.

8

"LET'S CALL YOUR MOM and check on our mail. It's been four months since we've received any," Molly said out of the blue. Thinking that she must know something that I didn't, I asked her just where among the coyotes and cactus might we find a telephone to make an international call. "San Carlos has telephones," she answered, as if she'd been born and raised there.

I pulled out the chart. San Carlos, a small coastal town on the Mexican mainland, was 160 miles away; a two-day sail each way at the very least in these fluky winds—just to check the mail! It was a wacky idea, but we had planned on visiting the mainland, and there really wasn't a lot of pressing business on our calendar.

I plotted a course for San Carlos, via Isla Raza, an island bird sanctuary where we wanted to witness the spectacle of 300,000 nesting gulls quarreling with 40,000 nesting terns.

Purely for show, we raised the jib and sailed the anchor out, hoisted the main, came about smartly, and sailed through the narrow channel out of Bahía Don Juan with a wave to our friends.

Raza was mesmerizing. An enormous mass of birds flew in perpetual circles above the small island like a swirling white cloud, while a never-ending screeching chorus rent the air, audible over a mile away.

We sailed completely around Raza, photographing the incredible bedlam, letting time slip away from us. It was unlikely that we could reach our intended anchorage before midnight, so we backtracked to a nearby island and anchored in a small cove in the lee of a rocky promontory.

Regardless of the existing weather conditions, we always

anchored as if a blow were imminent. On this particular night our methodical approach to anchoring served us well.

To be sure that the anchor was properly set, we routinely used a procedure that we termed the Thirds Rule:

Chain is released as the boat moves slowly astern until one-third of the desired scope is let out. At that point the engine is shifted into neutral and the anchor windlass is braked gently, allowing the anchor to begin to set with little risk of the chain fouling on the bottom. When two-thirds of the chain is out, the windlass is braked again and the engine is backed at half throttle for about 10 seconds to further set the anchor, then increased to full reverse while an anchoring range is observed. When we're satisfied that the anchor is not dragging at the two-thirds mark, we release the remaining third of the chain—the insurance third—and the boat drifts back.

This three-step method ensures that the anchor itself is securing the boat, and not the friction of the chain snaking over a rock or coral-strewn bottom, which is often the case if the entire scope is released at once. Using this system, *Swan*'s anchor has never dragged—ever.

In the middle of the night I sat bolt upright, startled from a sound sleep by an anxious call from Molly. *Swan* was hobbyhorsing alarmingly and a menacing sound of breaking waves sent a rush of adrenaline through me. I couldn't believe that I had been sleeping so soundly that I had not heard it. A glance at the depthsounder showed no significant change in the depth of the water, except for an expected tidal drop.

I grabbed a flashlight and sprang on deck. Molly switched on the spreader lights and started the engine while I made my way forward.

The wind had shifted 90 degrees. It was blowing hard from the north, dead into the cove. We were in deep enough water that the swells slid under us, but they were breaking dangerously close astern.

With each swell that passed, *Swan*'s bow lifted and the anchor chain snapped out of the water, bridging the valley between the seas. The chain's catenary was absorbing a tremendous shock load.

For a time I considered releasing the remaining chain and cutting the short length of "panic line" that secured the bitter end of the chain when it came through the hawse pipe. We could dive for it later. But the wind might blow for days from the north. I opted to winch in the anchor.

It was a slow process. As Molly motored slowly forward, I winched in a few feet of chain each time Swan's bow dipped into the valley between the swells when there was less strain on the rode.

When the anchor broke free, I gave Molly a hand signal to increase power, but I made no effort to bring it on board in the heavy surge.

A normal part of our anchoring procedure was to plot the compass course out of the harbor as a precaution for a nocturnal escape such as this, and post it on the chart. Molly steered, glued to the compass on this dark night, taking us seaward past extending reefs on both sides of the bay.

We continued for about 500 yards before I gave the signal to reverse the course, slowly, while I quickly winched the anchor on board with the seas astern.

Drenched with sweat and trembling from the combination of the adrenaline and exertion, I stood at the bow lamenting my decision to install a manual anchor windlass instead of a power-driven one. As the windlass and I grew older, the mistake was magnified (more in me than in the windlass).

The fact that a power winch stands ready at the bow is tacit encouragement to re-anchor in situations when the necessity to do so is marginal. We did, however, always make those decisions as if getting that great mass of iron up from the bottom was not the mule labor that it actually is. This probably accounts for our good anchoring record—and my fragile back.

On the positive side, the wind was perfect for the run to San Carlos.

Molly had been right about the existence of telephones at San Carlos. We squeezed into a humid, sweltering phone booth near the marina. I anticipated a linguistic ordeal as I dialed the number of the international operator, following the instructions written in Spanish on the telephone. A woman's voice, speaking excellent English with a Spanish accent, came on the line, "What country and party please?" I was so startled by this unexpected response in English that I mumbled my name and the country. Then, instead of referring to my mother by name, I childishly said I wanted to "call my mom collect." I was instantly embarrassed when she politely asked, "What is your mother's name?" I half expected her to follow with, "Does little Jimmy know Mommy's number?"

My mother had the important pieces of mail near the telephone for ready access if we called. Among these was a letter that had arrived two months earlier from the president of the publishing company who had asked to review my book manuscript. She read the letter to me while I was being distracted by a verbal barrage from Molly: "What's she saying? What did he say?"

After two readings of the letter, I had scribbled down the important information, the essence of which was that he liked the manuscript, he wanted to publish it, and he offered an advance payable upon my signing the contract.

When I hung up the phone, we danced around like a couple of loco gringos. A great deal of time, with ample portions of self-doubt, had been sandwiched between the writing of that first word and the receipt of a bona fide publishing offer.

I reached into my pocket and pulled out a wad of pesos and said to the mate with all of the drama I could muster, "I've got a hundred grand burning a hole in my pocket and the night is still young!" (There were 3000 pesos to the dollar.) It was a grand night.

Our next move was to get someplace where it would be reasonable to leave Molly alone on the boat, while I returned to the United States to do the necessary contract business. We did not want to attempt to complete it using the Mexican postal system.

San Felipe, on the Baja side, had a protected harbor, and it was only 120 miles from the California border with a highway leading north. On the downside, it was 300 miles northwest of San Carlos. We had sailed the wrong way from Don Juan.

It doesn't take long for a change in living conditions to change one's priorities. The fuel dock at the marina in San Carlos pumped clean fuel and had a hose with real water running through it. On most of the Baja California peninsula, diesel fuel and fresh water are scarce commodities that are usually brought on board in jerry jugs via the dinghy. We couldn't wait to get our hands on the water hose and give *Swan* her first freshwater bath in five months. At 0530 we moved the boat from the anchorage to the fuel dock, giving us a two-hour stint with the hose before the marina opened for business.

There was a bank, pharmacy, and a small grocery store within walking distance of the marina; a veritable center of commerce compared to Bahía de Los Angeles. After a small hassle, we cashed some traveler's checks at the one-horse bank and bought more groceries than we could carry, requiring a taxi ride to the marina.

Isla Tiburón, a large island 85 miles north of San Carlos was our immediate destination en route to San Felipe. Safe anchorage can be found in one of two bays at the southern tip of the island.

Tiburón was once the home of the fierce Seri Indians, who would have welcomed a visitor by turning him on a spit during their cannibal days. Fortunately, their descendants have mellowed into gentle souls who live simple lives, sustaining themselves from the bounty of the sea.

Swan reached northward under full sail in a light land breeze that held steady all day and throughout the night. We were especially grateful for this favorable wind on the return trip, because it had been fair coming over. It can't be on the nose all of the time!

It is early afternoon. The mountains of Tiburón are slowly changing from purple-gray to brown as we bear down on the island at six knots. The wind has shifted to the southwest, on the beam; we will anchor on the eastern side of the island, in Bahía Perros (Dog Bay). No hazards lie between us and the island. The water is deep. Tiburón is still two hours away. Old Sol blazes down, but it is cool under the sailing awning. This carefree sail epitomizes what we envisioned when we chose this nomadic way of life.

Molly appears at the companionway with iced tea, crackers, cheese, and jalapeño peppers. Within minutes I rub my eye and manage to burn my eyelid. Forty years of eating hot peppers and I still rub pepper juice in my eyes.

Molly opens James Michener's book, *Hawaii*. In an allusion to his wordiness I say, "In the beginning there was a barren hunk of lava in the Pacific." This engenders a negative response from the mate. She has read most of Michener's books and doesn't appreciate my unsolicited remarks.

I'm reading *The Grey Seas Under*, by Farley Mowat. His enormous writing talent always makes me envious. Only he can make a tale about a coal-burning salvage ship in the Western Ocean riveting.

Snap! The library atmosphere is replaced by the excitement of a strike on the starboard trolling line. Molly scoops up the snacks and books and puts them in the galley sink while I wind in the port fish line.

A golden-green fish flashes just beneath the surface, taking the line singing through the water fully to windward, where it bursts through the waves in a spectacular leap, clearing the water by more than its length. It's a four-foot dorado. Falling backward, it shakes its body violently in an effort to free itself from the tiny squid that has turned the tables on it. Now it dives, emerging a few seconds later in a powerful flying cartwheel—magically its color changes—it's now a sleek silver bullet with iridescent purple waves radiating down its sides.

This is our first dorado strike in the Sea of Cortez. The species migrate north into the sea as the summer wears on. They are a prize game fish. For pure fighting performance, pound for pound, the high-spirited dorado steals the show. These surface-feeding, deepwater fish are first-rate table fare— far and away our favorite.

Wearing leather gloves I begin to haul in the line, hand over hand, while Molly winds in the slack on the wooden reel. Suddenly the fish darts toward the boat. The line goes slack. I haul it in rapidly until I feel tension on the line—the fish is still hooked. Allowing the line to go slack is a quick way to lose a dorado.

As it nears the transom, the tired fish regains its will to fight. It dives under the boat, wrapping the line around the rudder shaft. I haul on the line and the fish is pulled under the boat—this will never do. Slowly I let the line slip around the shaft until the dorado is trailing behind the boat.

Tiburón looks very near. A 20-degree twist of Vane's neck and *Swan* falls off the wind. The boatspeed decreases. Tiburón is now two points on the port bow.

Molly manages to snag the submerged line with the boat hook. We bring the fish close enough to the transom to gaff it and get it on board. I roll it up in a towel. Our first dorado of the voyage is landed.

Few fish, even the magnificent dorado, can win a battle against a large double hook, 100-pound test stainless steel leader, and heavy shock-absorbing nylon line. This fish measures 52 inches in length.

We take in the reacher and approach Bahía Perros under the main alone.

Pelicans are not particularly bright, as birds go, but they seem to have a telepathic ability to sense the presence of a fish on board a boat, and their complete disregard for the rules of fair play, when fish are involved, is legendary. Several dozen of these long-beaked beggars surrounded *Swan* immediately as we anchored, and more arrived after we launched the dinghy. They were reinforced by a band of renegade diving boobies.

I have had a long and dismal relationship with seabirds. They seem to know instinctively that they will easily win any contest they have with me.

I am not one who sees a conspiracy behind every tree. I do not believe that a cabal of 12 Zurich bankers control the finances of the entire world, and I'd bet the farm that Oswald acted alone. But there have been just too many occasions, as we've sailed near some guano-encrusted rock populated by a motley group of seabirds, when the birds have suddenly stopped bickering amongst themselves, stared intently at me, then turned away and huddled together conspiratorially.

Molly cavalierly writes off my theory as absurd. It's easy enough for her to pooh-pooh my fears of a seabird conspiracy, because she hasn't been victimized like I have been on a regular basis by these web-footed, feathered bullies.

I sat in the dinghy cleaning the dorado with perhaps a hundred avian eyes riveted on me. The first fish entrails that I threw overboard were pounced upon by a thrashing blur of feathers. The birds were immediately emboldened by this delightful appetizer, and crowded around the dinghy with their beaks protruding over the gunnels as I boned the fish. My efforts to scare them away by shouting and threatening them with the knife had little effect. The two boobies assigned to distract me by jumping onto the transom were successful. In a flash of beak, a pelican whipped a long fillet out of the dinghy. It ran across the water dragging the piece of fish while furiously flapping its wings in a running battle for the prize with a few of its thieving mates.

I scooped up some water with a large stainless steel mixing bowl that was to contain the fillets, and threw the water in the faces of the closest birds that were pecking at the fish. Being diving birds, they weren't fazed for an instant. On the second scoop, the bowl slipped from my grasp and sank in 35 feet of murky water before I could react. I retreated to *Swan* with what was left of our fine fish.

According to the mate's periodic laments, there has never been another mixing bowl comparable to the one that I lost, and I am absolutely certain there never will be.

Swan's anchor was up well before sunrise. The cove was free from submerged hazards and fell away sharply into deep water. This enabled us to power safely into the channel between Tiburón and a neighboring island in the moonlight, to take advantage of the making tide.

Penetrating heat from the first rays of the rising sun gave promise of a scorcher. Not a breath of wind stirred, nor was there a cloud in the sky. The sea was glass. We rigged an awning and prepared ourselves for a long day of motoring. It had that look about it.

Fourteen hours of hot, tiresome motoring later, the sun mercifully set, snuffing out of the brain-piercing glare. I shut off the engine and *Swan* coasted to a stop. The sudden silence was almost audible. San Felipe seemed a long way off.

A skipjack tuna lay in the bottom of the cockpit. Landing it had provided a brief period of excitement on an otherwise monotonous day. I set about cleaning the fish. There wasn't a bird in sight—at least we had given the pelicans and boobies the slip.

In the stifling heat and humidity the sea looked inviting, but we had rules about that. We contented ourselves with bucket baths on the foredeck.

Not a breath of wind stirred. The engine had turned the cabin into a sauna. On this steamy night the cockpit would become our bedroom as well as the dining room.

To avoid the heat in the galley, Molly prepared sashimi; the first we had eaten since leaving Honolulu. She sliced an iced tuna fillet into small, thin pieces, and arranged them on a bed of shredded cabbage. Using chopsticks, we dipped the raw fish into a mixture of soy sauce and hot mustard.

Chilled pork and beans grown in the American heartland, garnished with cilantro, and a relish tray of sliced bell peppers, onions, tomatoes, and jalapeños served with an ice-cold Corona, rounded out this international supper on the sea.

Weariness from the long siege of motoring made an early night of it. We were stretched out in the cockpit as the stars began to appear in the evening twilight. I was thankful that we didn't need these old friends on this peaceful night. We knew where we were. *Swan* was in safe water, 20 miles from the nearest land.

I went below and switched on the anchor light, set the alarm clock for three hours, and put on a Hawaiian tape. *Song of the Islands*, one of my favorite songs, wafted across the tranquil waters. I tried to stay awake, but I never made it to the end of the song, and Molly never heard it at all.

At 0200, two alarm cycles later, a light breeze blew from

the northwest, directly out of San Felipe. But any wind was better than no wind. Close-hauled, flying the full main and the reacher, we eked out three knots, sailing 40 degrees off course to the northward.

Vane was having trouble holding the course. Normally he steered die-straight on this point of sail, even in light airs. His steering was sluggish and erratic, and I knew why. Barnacles were growing inside the submerged portion of the steering rudder shaft. They were restricting movement and chafing the dacron lines leading through the shaft to the servo that operated the steering rudder. Ordinarily I cleaned the tube when I dove to scrape the barnacles off the propeller. But we had been so preoccupied with hedonistic pursuits that I had neglected this maintenance chore.

San Felipe was 150 miles away. Neither Molly nor I had the slightest bit of enthusiasm for manually steering a compass course for 30 or 40 hours.

Because of the constant swell, it was very difficult to scrape off the growth at sea by diving. Removing the rudder from its mountings and hauling the unwieldy unit on board was the only reasonable way to do the job at sea. Then one faced the frustrating task of aligning the submerged rudder shaft with the thrust bearings to slide it back in place.

Our marriage, *Swan*'s transom, and my psyche still bear scars from having performed this task on a passage over a decade earlier.

The chart showed an anchorage at a small village on the mainland, La Libertad, 25 miles to the northeast, where we could clean the steering gear.

I was aware that this diversion could briefly delay the realization of my dream of seeing a book of my authorship in print. I was also cognizant of the fact, to my great and enduring annoyance, that the book-reading public had fared very well without any literary contributions from me, and they could probably hold out for another day or two.

We changed course for La Libertad.

Our arrival at the village created a stir. It was off the

beaten track, and very few cruising yachts ventured that far north.

Through binoculars we watched two young men scurry up a hill to a small, well-kept building with the Mexican flag flying smartly above it. Minutes later the militia fell out, armed and ready to defend Mexico's sacred soil against the imposing naval force that had entered the bay.

Down the hill they came. A squad of marines with rifles at port arms, led by an officer carrying a submachine gun and packing a side arm. Bringing troops with him was a gross case of overkill if I'd ever seen one.

They commandeered a fishing *panga* and the officer took a position at the bow like Washington crossing the Delaware with a Tommy Gun. In front of him a yellow dog hung over the prow, barking at the water. Four marines stood behind the officer, with the fisherman manning the outboard motor. The remainder of the squad milled about on the beach.

As the invincible force approached, I had an inkling of how Davy Crockett, Jim Bowie, and the boys must have felt during the final minutes at the Alamo.

> Flashed all their sabres bare—
> Flashed as they turned in air—
> Sab'ring the gunners there—

In the romance of the moment, my Walter Mitty mind confused a couple of wars.

Quit fooling with the fenders, Molly, and look up the Spanish words for "We surrender!"

When they were a short distance away, the officer gestured toward the port side. We frantically put over a phalanx of fenders to defend against 25 feet of jagged gunnel sidling up to *Swan*.

"Buenas tardes Capitan," I said, which probably elevated the officer's actual rank.

"Buenas tardes," he answered in a very official voice, but with a hint of a smile that belied his stern facade.

He stepped on board *Swan*, followed by two of his men.

109

The mangy dog, who had only one eye and an ugly scar where the missing eye had been, scrambled aboard under the lifelines and immediately began sniffing along the deck. It appeared that we had underestimated the level of sophistication of the boarding party, if their dog was trained to sniff out drugs.

The officer slung his submachine gun over his shoulder and we went below. He superficially examined our visas and ship's paper as he asked one word questions: Drugs? Alcohol? Weapons? I answered his questions with one word answers.

He glanced around the boat and his gaze fixed on a hammock strung above the settee in which we stored clothing. He thought the hammock was for a baby.

"Niños?" he said with a bright smile.

"No-no-no, no niños!" I said, while waving my hands back and forth in mock horror.

This elicited a laugh from him and his men, who were standing in the cockpit peering into the cabin, and the whole charade was over.

Molly opened her last six-pack of diet cola, which she had been hoarding, and a bag of potato chips. Her offerings were eagerly accepted by the officer, his men, and the fisherman.

The four-legged narc's one eye was riveted on the bag of chips. It was too much of a temptation for him and he stuck his nose in the bag. The fisherman yanked him through the lifelines and gave him a resounding whack that sent him crashing into the bilge. It wasn't much of a mystery how he had lost his eye.

We had given the dog too much credit. He belonged to the fisherman and was just a curious mutt who had jumped on board to check things out.

They thanked us for the snacks and we thanked them for their hospitality. They posed for a picture, then roared away with the dog hanging precariously over the prow, apparently having recovered from his misadventure on board a visiting yacht.

I had the steering gear operational before Molly had the rubber boot marks and mud removed from the non-skid.

As it turned out, the wind vane was of little value on the crossing. A dead calm had descended over the entire northern part of the sea, forcing us to motor almost the entire distance.

9

THERE WAS A LOT MORE to the San Felipe boat basin than met the eye—mainly silt. The harbor was a prime example of a pattern that is widely evident in Mexico—the construction of public projects with little effort expended in long-term maintenance.

At low water, the jetty-enclosed harbor drained dry in tides that ranged as high as 23 feet in this part of the Sea of Cortez. In the extreme outer part of the basin, where tidal currents prevented silt from building up, there was a small area that could accommodate a few boats.

Swan squeezed into a corner of this area in company with a cruising trimaran and a nondescript vessel named *Shark Bait*.

It was like anchoring an elevator. At high tide *Swan* had about 18 feet of water under her keel, and at low tide she was buried in the mud. We set two bow anchors at a 50-degree angle and tied the stern to the quay with a "Y" bridle constructed of three 100-foot lines. The anchor lines were taut at high tide, and sloppy to the point of uselessness at low water. It didn't matter though, because at low tide a bulldozer couldn't have moved the boat with her keel and rudder stabbed in the mud. We never ran the engine to charge the systems at low tide because of the danger of sucking silt into the cooling system.

After supper, Molly was lying in the bunk reading and I was fiddling with a calculator. I made a few apprehensive sounds which caused Molly to think that something was wrong.

"What's the matter?" she said.

"If my calculations are correct," I said with concern in my

voice, "if we bog down another six inches, the boat may not have enough natural buoyancy to suck her out of the mud when the tide comes in."

She thought I was serious for a moment, until I added, "It might be a good idea to close the port above your head so seawater won't pour in on your face."

Her dark Italian eyes flashed when she realized I was kidding and she said, "I don't think that's one bit funny. You're getting ready to run off to the United States and leave me here alone in this ridiculous harbor on this cotton-picking floating yo-yo!"

With that she snapped off the light and turned her back to me.

I lay there thinking of the terrible price I have paid over the years because of my cute little tricks.

Early the next morning I rowed ashore on the flood tide with two empty water jugs. A friendly young fellow filled the five-gallon jugs with water from a tanker truck that was parked on the wharf. Pure drinking water was not piped to the boat basin. The charge was 1500 pesos for each jug; a fair price considering the circumstances.

A few hours later I rowed ashore again with four water jugs. Twenty gallons would top off the tanks. On this trip, a fact of life was made rudely clear to me: even though San Felipe was 120 miles from the United States, it was essentially a border town.

Near the tanker truck was a dilapidated building with an overhanging roof covering a low porch. Seated at a round table on the porch were four men and the fellow who had sold the water to me earlier. They were eating ceviche with their fingers from a large bowl in the center of the table and drinking beer. Empty beer bottles were strewn about on the porch.

I stood in the noonday sun near the water truck. The young fellow nodded to me, but the men ignored me. Ill at ease, I finally greeted them in Spanish. A fat slob of a man who was wearing dark glasses, and had greasy, slicked-back hair, looked up from his food long enough to grunt some unintelligible sound. The others gave me a quick glance and said nothing.

These men were a world away from the gentle and friendly people at Bahía de Los Angeles.

My instincts told me to gather up the jugs and leave. But I didn't want to leave Molly on the boat with partially filled water tanks.

"Agua," I said, while pointing at the water spigot on the truck. The fat man, who was the obvious boss of the group, looked up and grunted "Si," and nodded toward the truck.

It was foolish of me not to verify the price. I assumed it would be the same as before, and I filled the four water jugs.

As I was filling the last jug, two small, barefooted boys walked timidly up to me and pointed at the water faucet. I filled a plastic dipper and they each took a drink and said, "Gracias".

I walked over to the table to pay for the water and asked the portly one, "Cuanto es?"

"Sixty-thousand pesos, twenty bucks U.S.," he said without looking up. He even knew American slang.

The young fellow glanced at me and quickly turned away. He was obviously embarrassed. Sixty-thousand pesos was a dollar a gallon, ten times the price I had paid earlier!

"Too much," I said. I didn't mention the amount I had paid for the first two jugs because it would probably have caused trouble for the young man. He had most likely sold the water to me at the local fishermen's price.

I laid 20,000 pesos on the table. The boss waved at it with the back of his hand in exaggerated disgust. He didn't respond when I asked him if he would put the water back in the tank. I asked him a second time. He ignored the question again.

My alternatives to paying the rip-off price weren't very good. If I dumped the water on the ground I would probably end up paying for it, or lose the jugs, or get roughed up, or possibly all three.

A ladder was leaning against the truck. I picked up a jug and climbed the ladder to pour the water back into the tank. They let me climb to the top, knowing that the filler cap was padlocked.

I have never been accused of being overly tolerant. I backed

down the ladder, seething with anger. That fat son-of-a-bitch!
I'll . . . Suddenly, I remembered an expression of a friend of
mine: "Don't let your alligator mouth outweigh your hum-
mingbird ass." I wasn't 25 anymore, and even if I were, there
were four of them; I was in a foreign country, and the last thing
we needed was a feud with a bunch of punk hoodlums, especially in view of the fact that Molly would be alone on the
boat.

I calmed myself and reopened negotiations. We eventually
settled on 45,000 pesos, to which I added 5000 pesos for the
"muchacho's agua." Fat boy knew immediately that I was trying to get in a last moral jab: an American buying water from a
Mexican to give to some thirsty Mexican children. He would
have none of it.

After pushing the 5000 peso note back and forth a few
times, I shoved it in my pocket, patted it, and said, "Tequila."
This brought forth a little self-conscious laughter from the
men.

It also presented an opportunity to ease the tension. They
offered me a beer and some ceviche, which I accepted. After
some polite small talk, I thanked them for the beer and the
young fellow helped me load the jugs in the dinghy. He was a
good kid. With a wink, I slipped him the 5000 peso note.

I rowed mechanically back to the boat, trying to rationalize
the fact that I had stooped to appeasement. One does what one
has to do—Molly wouldn't be harassed. I had purchased the
peace for 45,000 pesos and a little piece of my self-esteem. I felt
like the cruising equivalent of Neville Chamberlain.

I hadn't the foggiest idea how I was going to get to Calexico, a small California border town from where I hoped to conduct the book contract business with the publisher.

With a copy of my manuscript tucked in my suitcase, I
walked into a small bus station in the heart of San Felipe. A
thermometer on the wall read 112 degrees.

By chance, a northbound bus was leaving in two hours. I
purchased a ticket and sat down on a bench next to a man who

looked at me while mopping his forehead and said, "Caliente."
I didn't know the Spanish words for: "You've got that right."

The station was an oasis compared to the bus. I sat on the
back seat of the crowded bus as it rumbled through the desert,
shielding my face with my hands from the hot air blasting
through the windows. The wind actually burned my finger-
nails.

The young lad sitting next to me looked like he was about
to perish. I rummaged through my bag and brought out a bottle
of grapefruit juice wrapped in a towel, still cold from *Swan's* refrigerator. I offered the boy a drink. His eyes brightened and he
took a polite little sip. I pointed to a spot about halfway down
the bottle and he took a man-sized swig as if he were in a
Gatorade commercial on television.

Time dragged on until, at last, we reached Mexicali. My
young friend gave me a feeble wave and a wan smile, and disappeared into the crowd at the curb.

Mexicali is a short distance from the border, but too far to
walk. I needed a taxi.

Gaudily painted taxicabs lined the littered street in front of
the bus station. Several taxi drivers converged on me as I
stepped off the bus. I divided everything they said by three: the
kilometers to the border; the standard fare; the children they
were supporting—everything.

One of the most pleasurable moments in my life was when
I walked into the air-conditioned U.S. Immigration and Customs building in my sweat-soaked shirt. I stood in the center of
the room, basking in the cool, dry air while two customs agents
stared impatiently at me. The room was empty except for me
and the two officials. It was the first time that I could remember actually wanting to linger in a bureaucratic establishment,
and the first time that I could recall bureaucrats being anxious
to attend to my affairs. They processed me through the formalities with uncommon efficiency, and I was standing outside on a
steamy California sidewalk far too quickly for my liking.

It soon became apparent that Calexico was not the place to
do the business—there was too little "Cal" and too much
"exico." I caught a Greyhound bus to nearby El Centro and

rented an off-track motel room for $16 a night. It was air-conditioned, my only priority.

I lay sprawled across the bed drinking a beer and eating a cold burrito, idly wondering if this was how Tom Clancy got started.

"Oh for goodness sake," was my mother's response on the telephone when I told her that I was in California—and yes, I was being careful . . . Over the years she had grown accustomed to being unsure what country her second-born and his wife were currently occupying at any given moment.

She had spoken with the publisher on the telephone a few times since I had last talked with her, and she related to me what had transpired. This helped alleviate the hesitancy I often feel when making introductory phone calls.

It was an unnecessary concern, as the informal tone and friendly words of Lothar Simon, the President of Sheridan House Inc., dispelled any feelings of apprehension that I might have had.

My regard for the U.S. Postal Service was greatly enhanced during my stay in El Centro. Via Express Mail, the contract business was completed very efficiently, and I was on a bus back to the border in three days. *By Way of the Wind* was no longer a book manuscript in limbo. It was in the process of becoming a reality.

I renewed our six-month visas at the Mexican Consulate in Calexico and spent longer than I had anticipated shopping for a long list of items at those big, wonderful, American supermarkets and discount stores.

It was well into the afternoon when I lugged my bulging bag through the border crossing, hailed a taxi, and rode through the streets of Mexicali to the bus terminal.

A long line of people with bundles, bags, and babies snaked across a stiflingly hot room from a ticket counter. Please don't let that be the bus-to-San-Felipe line, I hoped as I walked toward an official-looking man at an adjacent counter. He more than confirmed my worst suspicions. The seats on the San Felipe bus were sold out. The line was for tickets to *stand in the aisle*. And it was the last bus of the day.

I dug a map of Baja California out of my suitcase and marked a spot at a place well outside of town where the road forked; one road leading south and the other to mainland Mexico. I gulped down two large glasses of lemonade at a taco stand, bought a carton of orange juice for later, and braced myself for the taxi negotiations.

Driver, after perusal of map: "Fifty-five thousand pesos, is good for you."

Me: "Twenty-thousand pesos, es muy bueno usted."

Driver gasps, rolls eyes—on the verge of cardiac arrest: "Forty-thousand—mucho gasolina."

Me, while edging toward another taxi: "Me poor gringo— 30,000, no mas."

Driver shakes head sadly—whipped dog look—personifies the very essence of defeat: "OK Señor . . . OK"

We shook hands and he threw my suitcase into the trunk. I thought I heard glass break. I tried not to visualize what a broken quart jar of spaghetti sauce might look like in the midst of white underwear.

After a longer ride than I had anticipated, the driver stopped a mile or so beyond the fork in the road at the foot of a small rise where the taxi could be turned around. I tipped him 6000 pesos, which instantly reestablished favorable Mexican/American relations. He drove away, and I suddenly felt very much alone and vulnerable.

I sat down on the parched ground at the edge of a ditch beside the road and removed my shoes. In one shoe I placed six $100 bills that I had withdrawn from an American bank, and in the other I put some large peso notes and my Visa card; leaving enough cash in my wallet to make things credible if I ran into banditos.

I took a file folder from a side pouch on my suitcase. When opened, the large felt-penned words "San Felipe" could be seen a fair distance away. I had made it for an eventuality such as this.

To keep the odds even, I had made the decision to hitchhike vehicles with only one occupant. It was something I would do anywhere, not just in Mexico.

My situation didn't seem very promising. During a 15-minute period only two cars and the jam-packed San Felipe bus passed by.

A truck approached, visually distorted in the shimmering heat rising from the highway. When it was about 100 yards from me I could distinguish the forms of three people in it and I turned away. A moment later I was startled by the sound of wheels on gravel. The driver had swerved the truck off the highway onto the shoulder of the road, apparently to scare me. This was accomplished to the utmost.

I leaped into the ditch, dragging my suitcase behind me as the truck thundered past with a man hanging out of the window laughing and pounding the door with his fist. I shouted some words that called into question the legitimacy of his birth, which was a foolish thing to do considering my lonely situation.

I stood there in the oppressive heat, thinking about the unpleasant attitudes in border towns; about the sun's alarming westward progress, and whether or not rattlesnakes really do try to cuddle up with you at night.

It was pointless to walk, but I wanted to see what lay over the hill. When I reached the top of the rise, I was dumbfounded to see what appeared to be a taco stand on the opposite side of the road about 300 yards away, surrounded by nothingness.

It was just too preposterous. It reminded me of a scene in an old Abbott and Costello movie when the two of them were lost in the desert. Costello was standing knee-deep in sand, trying in vain to grab an ice-cream soda at a mirage soda fountain before the illusion disappeared.

I crossed the road thinking that perhaps two tacos and two tall glasses of heavily iced lemonade would be about right for starters.

What had appeared at a distance to be a small stand was actually a cart affair with a flimsily constructed canopy. The cart had two tongues that apparently were for harnessing an animal. There was no animal in sight.

Standing by the cart in the shade of the cover was an old man with a weathered face who stared intently at me as I approached him. He acknowledged my greeting with a nod and mumbled something. Instead of tacos and ice-cold lemonade, there were cucumbers. The cart was chock-full of big, green cucumbers. Nothing else—just cucumbers.

What in the world was he doing here? How could it possibly be a viable thing? And where was his beast of burden? It was all so bizarre.

I couldn't remember the Spanish word for "horse," so I pointed toward the wagon tongues and asked, "Donde?" (where). He looked at the tongues, and then back at me with a puzzled expression, then looked around nervously. Again I pointed at the tongues and repeated the word "Donde?" and made the sound of a horse whinny. This caused the old man to throw his hands in the air and draw back sharply from me. It was such a comical reaction that I spontaneously laughed, which added to his alarm.

At this point I am sure he thought that I was either stark raving mad, or a reincarnated fugitive from the glue factory. I doubt that it would have surprised him if I had hitched myself to his wagon and hauled it off down the highway.

I had inadvertently frightened him, which distressed me. The state of affairs was such that any attempt that I might have made to ease his fears would only have made things worse. Still, I felt compelled to do something.

With an air of casual sanity, I picked up a large cucumber and held up a 1000 pesos. He nodded his head, but wasn't about to reach over the cart for the money. I could hardly blame him. I laid 2000 pesos on the cart, an extra 1000 for his pain and suffering, and walked across the road, trying with little success to suppress the humorous vision of the old guy jumping backward so nimbly.

He never took his eyes off me for a second as I stood by the side of the road eating the cucumber with a poorly concealed grin on my face. He probably thought a carrot would have suited me better.

About the time that I was getting very anxious about my

predicament, a pickup truck approached with one person in it. I held up the sign and the truck slowed to a stop. The driver, a middle-aged man, motioned for me to get in. I removed the carton of orange juice from my bag before I put it in the back of the truck.

It was most likely my imagination, but as we drove away I thought I heard a sigh of relief emanating from somewhere near the cucumber cart.

The fellow who picked me up worked as a fireman in California. He was a Mexican, born in San Felipe, and spoke excellent English. He was in the process of building a retirement home in San Felipe.

We split the orange juice and swapped a few war stories, and near sundown we arrived at the harbor where *Swan* lay at anchor. Talk about relief!

He adamantly refused payment for the ride. When he left, I opened the suitcase. It looked like a hog had been slaughtered in it. I gathered up two T-shirts that were saturated with spaghetti sauce and glass shards, and took the whole mess to the nearest rubbish can.

As I walked along the jetty, I could almost taste the giant margarita that I was thinking about.

10

THE SCORCHING HEAT WAVE that had lasted for two weeks could not have come at a worse time. The occasional sea breeze was blocked by the jetties, and the tidal waters were heated as they rolled in over the sunbaked flats. *Swan*'s hull absorbed heat from the water, raising the cabin temperature significantly. The sweltering conditions added yet another unpleasant element to our overall impression of San Felipe; an impression that didn't need any additional negatives.

But there was much to talk about. Molly wanted to know every detail of my trip. As the last rays of the sun faded into twilight, we repaired to the pool deck, aft, for cocktails.

The descent to *Swan*'s pool deck is less elegant than we would prefer. It is accomplished by climbing down the transom, using Vane's support frames as a ladder. Two tethered fenders provided partially submerged seating.

Sitting astride the fenders, with frosty margaritas in long-stemmed plastic glasses balanced precariously on the steering rudder, we enjoyed the tepid, though relatively cool comfort of the water as I related to Molly my adventures in the hinterlands of Mexico. The part about the cucumber cart had to be told twice.

Having had quite enough of the northern part of the sea, we were anxious to get back to our base area, Don Juan, and the village at Bahía de Los Angeles; and perhaps, enjoy a period of non-eventfulness. We brought in the spiderweb of mooring lines at first light, and motored south on a mirror sea.

An otherwise monotonous siege of powering was enlivened by a chance encounter with some roving aquatic mammals, a snapping fish, and two diving boobies.

Whale sightings are commonplace in the Sea of Cortez, but these gigantic animals are always a wonder to behold, regardless of how often one sees them. A pod of four or five finback whales were crossing at right angles to our course, about 500 yards in front of us. We altered course in an attempt to get close enough to photograph them.

Molly was steering and I was standing in the stern manipulating the two trolling lines like a puppeteer, trying to prevent a pair of diving boobies from hitting the lures. Apparently the action of the plastic squid was irresistible to a sleek, silver barracuda. It hit one of the lures, which further excited the birds.

Several dolphins picked that moment to make a grand entrance into the scene. They made crisscross passes in front of *Swan*'s bow, with a young one leaping completely out of the water from sheer exuberance.

I quickly hauled in the fish, hand over hand, but not fast enough. As I swung the barracuda on board, a booby hit the other lure and hooked itself.

Fortunately we were motoring, which enabled us to stop quickly. I gently pulled the squawking bird in and lifted it on board. When I removed the hook from its beak it gave me a painful peck on the wrist as its way of thanking me for my humane efforts. The ingrate then focused its tunnel vision on the barracuda, but seemed to have second thoughts about tangling in a shipboard battle with the needle-toothed fish that was lying on the cockpit sole, snapping its jaws open and closed like an agitated dog. The bird then astounded us by suddenly closing its eyes and nodding off.

By this time the whale photo-op was gone and the dolphins had deserted us; so we settled for a picture of the booby, who had awakened from its brief nap and was standing in the coils of fish line, looking wistfully at the forbidden feast lying in the bottom of the cockpit.

The difficulties that we had experienced obtaining fresh water during the previous few weeks had demonstrated the value of having a watermaker on board a cruising yacht.

When we built *Swan* in the early 1970s, a bulky, fuel-guzzling distillation plant was the only option one had for desalinating seawater. I don't recall the term "reverse-osmosis" even being used in those days. Sufficient tankage and a means of collecting rainwater was our solution to the problem. Fresh-water making was something that had been handled splendidly by the Almighty throughout the ages, and we had every reason to believe this generous practice would continue. A cruising sailor's task was to collect, preserve, and conserve this precious liquid, and hope that the benevolent Deity would direct a moisture-laden squall in his direction when the water tanks had gotten to the critical stage on a long passage.

That system had worked fairly well; like the horse and buggy had worked fairly well. We regretted our mistake of not installing a reverse-osmosis desalinator when we were fitting out in California. One adjusts to living with an inconvenience, and puts up with it out of habit.

Watermakers aside, *Swan*'s conventional water supply system was more than adequate. It contained some useful features that are often missing in newer boats.

The forward tank held 83 gallons of fresh water, and the capacity of the amidships tank was 34 gallons. For integrity reasons, the tanks were independently plumbed. Water could be transferred from the large tank to the small tank, which held the cooking and drinking water, by means of a hose that attached to the galley faucet.

Chlorine bleach was added to the drinking tank at a ratio of one ounce per 20 gallons of water, which eliminated any harmful bacteria and prevented algae growth. Particles, and the taste and odor of chlorine were removed from the water by an in-line carbon filter. This super chlorination/dechlorination process allowed us to take on water of questionable purity in remote parts of the world.

A hand-operated pump drew water from the drinking tank. This promoted conservation, because one pumps only what one needs. An electric pump delivered water from the forward tank to the head and the galley sink. The system could be operated either on an automatic demand mode, or on a manually operated, momentary switch mode. In port we used the demand system, just as a faucet in a house is used, and at sea we used the momentary switch mode. The latter system prevented the pump from activating from pressure loss should a leak occur, or a faucet be left on.

Salt water is the one unlimited commodity at a sailor's disposal. With this in mind, we did not limit its use by employing a slow-delivery, hand-operated pump. With a flick of a switch, salt water flowed from a galley faucet at four gallons per minute, at a small cost of electrical power, leaving both hands free. We used salt water to wash dishes, clean fish, cook foods (if we were in unpolluted waters), and for many other jobs. Dishes received a final freshwater rinse.

Even the most state-of-the-art water system on a cruising boat should include a high-delivery saltwater tap at the galley sink. Parenthetically, Joy, Ivory, and Dawn detergents lather well in salt water.

If we were to build another boat (not really, Molly, you can unpack your bags) it would have *Swan*'s water system with the addition of a desalinator. If the watermaker packed up just west of Cocos-Keeling, it would only be an inconvenience, not a pressing problem.

Through all of the torrid weather, the refrigeration system had performed perfectly. It, more than anything else, had made life bearable in the trying conditions.

Having an efficient refrigeration unit on board contributed greatly to our longevity in a way of life that can exact stiff payment in hardship as the price of freedom. At the outset, we approached the transition from life on the land to life on the water with the premise that the amenities we enjoyed in our home would not suddenly become unimportant once the dock lines were slipped—and they didn't.

For some mysterious reason, rational people who have lived all of their lives enjoying the pleasure and convenience of refrigeration, suddenly try to convince themselves that they will be able to cruise aboard a boat for years on end, often in tropical conditions, and scarcely miss this wonderful enhancement to living.

I believe that it would be far easier to live without refrigeration in a house on land than on a long-distance cruising yacht. At least on land, fresh vegetables and refrigerated foods are available on a daily basis at the corner grocery store.

When I cover this subject at cruising seminars, I offer a standard test to those people who are in a quandary about refrigeration. I suggest that they unplug their refrigerator at home for the three summer months. If, at the end of that period, they feel that it hasn't been too great a sacrifice, they will probably get along quite nicely without refrigeration on their ocean cruise.

Within reason, one cannot overbuild a marine refrigeration system, or keep it too simple. From my observations, the most common causes of problems are inadequate or the wrong type of insulation, overly complicated installations, vibration-caused failures, and electrically driven compressors that place too great a drain on the storage batteries.

"Marine refrigeration" has become synonymous with "headache," which need not be the case. I designed and built the engine-driven compressor/cold-plate refrigeration unit on *Swan* with an attention to detail normally reserved for spacecraft systems. It was ruggedly constructed and was the epitome of simplicity, operating with no instrumentation other than a household thermometer.

Closed-cell polyurethane foam insulation was used, well in excess of the minimum requirements. The insulation was covered with heat reflecting foil and a heavy plastic moisture barrier. In short, I built a proper marine refrigeration system, *then* built a galley around it. My efforts have been amply rewarded by the nearly flawless running of the system for 15 years.

The compressor running time varied with the ambient temperature. For example, in the cool waters off the Cape of Good Hope we ran the engine as little as 40 minutes per day, while at San Felipe it required 40 minutes of running, morning and evening. On average, one hour of running time was sufficient to maintain frozen foods indefinitely and produce two trays of ice cubes each day.

On several occasions we left the boat unattended for periods up to three days with frozen food on board. Before leaving, we ran the refrigeration compressor for three hours and covered the frozen food with a towel and a wool blanket. No food was ever lost.

In my opinion an ice box is not a viable option for a blue-water yacht. Foods cannot be frozen, and ice is often unavailable in remote regions, to say nothing of the nuisance factor.

Not only does refrigeration make life more pleasant, it also affords the means to take advantage of windfalls. We sailed across the South Atlantic with the freezer stuffed with lobster that we had trapped along the coast of Namibia.

It has been my impression that people who elect to "get along" without refrigeration aboard their floating home (not a weekend sailer) do not begin missing it after a few months have elapsed—a few hours is closer to the mark—or from that very first moment when they look askance at the opened jar of mayonnaise.

But, if one were faced with the stark choice to go cruising without refrigeration or not to go at all, I would shout: GO! GO! GO!

It was a delight to see that the nucleus of the "fleet" was anchored at Don Juan when we sailed into the bay. As parties and potlucks played a large role in life in the hurricane hole, a party was planned for that evening. The bash was held on board *Swan*, and for the occasion we flew the burgee of the Baja Howling Coyote Society.

Membership in the society was not something handed out willy-nilly like ambassadorships; it was *earned*. To be admitted into this elite society, one had to develop a coyote howl that could deceive the uninitiated crew of a newly arrived yacht into believing that the band of real coyotes that inhabit the area had descended on the anchorage. The mating howl was, of course, strictly forbidden.

With a litmus test of this stringency, it was understandable that membership in the society was confined to a small group. The crews of only four boats were full-fledged members: Bruce and Reta Lombardi on *Misty Dawn Two*; Terry and Ingrid

Thompson on *Kodiak*; Bob and Annemarie Hutton on *Neptune's Gold*; and the crew of *Swan*. Ingrid received special honors for designing and sewing the society burgees on a hand-cranked sewing machine.

The remaining weeks of the hurricane season passed quickly, with our time taken up diving on the reefs, fishing, gathering the oysters and clams that were in abundance, and exploring nearby islands.

During this high-stress period I found time to teach an informal class on celestial navigation. This ancient art enjoyed a renaissance among a few skippers who were soon to set sail for the South Pacific, and their confidence in electronic navigation had been shaken by the melting down of a few high-tech systems.

They were familiar with the basic concepts of the subject, which put the instruction on a level that was enjoyable to teach. In the evening the voices of the born-again navigators could be heard echoing across the bay: "Arcturus is at 51 degrees! There's Deneb straight above the inlet!" I would contribute to this celestial discord with wonderfully authentic coyote howls.

It was time to move on. With reluctance we sailed out of Don Juan for the last time. We crossed the bay to the village to say goodbye to our friends and to gamble one more time on the arrival of the phantom vegetable truck. While we waited for the truck, we filled our water tanks from a hillside well and washed our clothes.

There are few things in a cruising sailor's everyday life as intimidating as a large bag of dirty laundry. We eased this drudgery considerably by never having a bag of dirty laundry. Instead we had a sort of perpetual washing system.

Pre-soaking the clothing was the key. We placed two five-gallon buckets, half filled with fresh water, in one of the large cockpit lockers; one for colored clothing and the other for white. Soap was added to each bucket, with a *small* quantity of bleach mixed into the one designated for white clothing. When we took off a garment, it was placed directly into the appropriate bucket. Occasionally we agitated the soaking clothes, unless we had planned our itinerary so poorly that the pounding of the boat took care of the agitation problem, in which case lids were snapped on the buckets.

On laundry day we scrubbed out any stubborn stains from the garments and wrung the soapy water out by doubling the article of clothing around a shroud. This method of wringing allows you to twist the item in one direction with both hands, effectively removing the water.

Each bucket was then filled with fresh water as a first and second rinse, and the clothes rinsed and wrung out. We made an effort to collect the water if water was scarce. Then we added soap and bleach to the leftover rinse water, which served as the next week's wash cycle.

On big wash days, when the bedding was washed, we used a special drying rig made of one-quarter inch nylon line. It was an A-frame affair with multiple cross-lines spliced to the vertical support lines, roughly two feet apart. The vertical lines were secured to the toerail on each side of the boat about six feet aft of the mast. The top of the "A" was attached to the main halyard. Towels and sheets were doubled exactly in half on the cross lines and fastened with clothespins as the rig was raised one tier at a time.

This method of drying laundry was used only while at anchor, when the bow naturally pointed into the wind; and for reasons of aesthetics, we used it only in remote places.

On a breezy day it was marvelously efficient, and created a sight that would have put a clipper ship topman's heart in his throat. We looked like a square-rigger hove up with all her tops'ls blown out.

The passage south to La Paz was a pleasant series of day sails running before the prevailing northerly wind, with stops at our favorite anchorages along the way.

During our eight-month stay in the Sea of Cortez we sailed 1600 miles; lugged some 850 gallons of fresh water in five-gallon jugs over rock jetties, mud flats, and through breaking surf; caught 10 dorado, numerous tuna, razor-toothed barracuda, a ton of bass, trigger fish, snapper, halibut, and a variety of puffer fish and other weird denizens that inhabit those waters; gathered buckets and buckets of clams, scallops, oysters and conch; rowed 40 to 50 miles; anchored 130 plus times, which converted to approximately *three miles* of chain, all brought in with the hand-operated windlass or other brute means; swam and snorkeled nearly every day; ate a three-foot stack of tortillas; consumed two gallons of salsa, and even found time to drink a margarita or two, if one can imagine that.

La Paz was a major provisioning stop. We filled four shopping carts at the Federal Supermarket in the center of town, and took advantage of the modern facilities at Marina de La Paz to tend to *Swan*'s needs. It was also where a sad aspect of the cruising life took place: saying goodbye to friends, many of whom we would probably never see again. In the sentimentality of the moment, I owned up to the truth about the recipe for the "Hawaiian Mai Tai" cocktails I had prepared with such hoopla and fanfare at Don Juan: cheap tequila mixed with Tang and slices of lime.

With our port clearance in order, we sailed through the Canal de San Lorenzo and set a course that would take us to Socorro in the Revilla Gigedo Islands, 250 miles south of Cabo San Lucas.

In the late afternoon the northerly wind faltered. We motorsailed 10 miles along the coast to Los Frailes, the anchorage that we had failed to reach before nightfall when we had first entered the sea. This time we won the race with the setting sun.

We stayed at Los Frailes for two days waiting for a fair wind. The bottom fell away sharply from the beach. It was 50 feet deep off *Swan*'s stern and fishing was excellent. I had just hooked a pan-size porgy when I heard Molly exclaim, "Well I see our investments took a nosedive."

I hooked the reel of the fishing rod under the mainsheet and put the porgy on hold.

Miss Busyness had been squaring away the forepeak and had found the financial section of the *Los Angeles Times* that I had foolishly left in my suitcase upon my return from California. It would have been a kind turn of fate indeed had the newspaper suffered the same destruction by spaghetti sauce that befell the T-shirts.

Molly was sitting on the settee wearing her Benjamin Franklin-style glasses, reading the stock market quotes and delivering a running commentary as if it were hot news off the wire. I felt compelled to explain the subtle distinction between a technical correction in the market and a "nosedive!"

Our stock losses were, at least for the moment, only paper losses. However, it was a different story with our other investments.

Interest rates had dropped two full percentage points since I had inaugurated my grand strategy of short-term investments. These investments, the very ones that were supposed to keep the cruising kitty fat and healthy by taking advantage of the anticipated interest/inflation upward spiral were working in reverse! They were locking in every interest rate cut that the Federal Reserve Bank initiated to stimulate the stagnant economy. George's steady hand on the tiller of the Ship of State was so steady that I wondered if it had a pulse!

Once again, nothing was working according to my plan— so I resorted to the old familiar standby: "Those doom-and-gloom Harvard economists and the tax-and-spend Democrats have the President by the jugular."

The mate abruptly folded up the paper and went back to her cleaning before I had a chance to start in on the liberal media and the high-handed tactics of the Japanese.

Swan pushed southward, flying the jib and reefed mainsail in a fresh nor'wester. In the early evening the wind shifted due west, then abruptly died with the land still in sight. We motored for three hours to eliminate the discouraging possibility of the land being discernible at sunrise. It's one thing to determine by navigational means that very little progress has been made, and quite another to meet the day with the indisputable fact staring you in the face.

Swan lay becalmed on this balmy, moonless night. We sat in the dark cockpit watching a cruise ship approach from the west. We were feeling a bit low in spirits, thinking of our friends and missing them already.

The ship passed very close, a quarter of a mile at most. It was ablaze with lights, like a floating carnival. We could see people moving about, and could almost hear the laughter and festive popping of champagne corks. This perceived gaiety did nothing to alter my nostalgic mood, but it sparked Molly.

Enough of this gloominess! It was time to join the party!

She broke out the salted queso, our favorite Mexican cheese made from goat's milk, and uncorked a bottle of red wine she had bought at the Federal Surplus Store in La Paz with the memorable remark: "It should be good, it cost 6000 pesos!" (Molly really loved those big numbers).

The cheese was delightful as usual, and my nostalgia vanished completely when that first drink of wine went down—all that was missing was the olive oil and Italian seasoning.

Light, fickle winds plagued the crossing to Socorro. Lackluster progress, as we were soon to discover, would be more the rule than the exception on our passage south to Panama, with an occasional gale thrown in to alleviate boredom.

On the morning of the fourth day we raised the island. Even though it was a relatively short distance from the mainland, the materialization of land on the horizon was still captivating. The verdant mountain slopes of Socorro were a welcome change from the barren hills of the Baja peninsula.

Socorro, at 19°N 111°W, lies in the path of many of the hurricanes that are spawned on the west coast of Mexico and spin off westward into the Pacific Ocean, inundating the island with rainfall as they pass over the mountains that tower 3700 feet above sea level.

The absence of outlying hazards makes the approach to the anchorage at the southeastern tip of the island a safe and easy one.

To our immense delight, Steve and Pat Strand, whom we had first met at Don Juan, were there on their sailboat, *Danzante*.

Swan underwent a full-blown boarding by a small squad of Mexican Marines from a garrison on the island. While impressive, the guardians of Socorro lacked the bravado of the La Libertad boarding party.

We were taken by jeep up the mountain to meet the Post Commandant. With Steve's fluent Spanish greasing the wheels of diplomacy, we were graciously granted the run of the island, the use of the laundry facilities, and all of the fresh water we needed from their desalination plant.

Although the water temperature of the ocean was a bit low for diving without a wet suit, the outstanding visibility, as much as 125 feet, and the rare species of sea life that live in the canyon-like inlets, made it too good an opportunity to pass up. Frequent rests on the hot lava rocks at the base of the sheer cliffs replaced the body heat lost during the dives.

The laundry facilities were straightforward—vintage 1850s. We rubbed and beat the clothing on slab basins under the shade of a palapa, using brackish water drawn from a nearby well. Lines were strung between trees to dry the clothes, and we draped the sheets over bushes on the hillside. More than once the girls mentioned that the conditions were "far better than what we're used to."

The "Magic Ball" worked its peculiar brand of magic for the children of the island. I have carried it with me everywhere for 30 years—it's invisible, and impossible to lose. It instantly overcomes language barriers. When it is elaborately inflated and tossed into the air with a flourish, all eyes follow it. When it is caught in a paper bag with an audible thump the reaction of the children is always the same: wide-eyed wonderment.

As Ringling Brother's "Greatest Show On Earth" doesn't come to town every day on Socorro, we soon had a growing band of curious kids following us tentatively through the village. Their timidity vanished when Molly opened the bag of candy she carried for times like these.

With the freezers stuffed with loaves of coarse, dark bread from the post bakery, the two boats sailed on the morning breeze. We sailed in tandem for most of the day, but toward evening *Swan* chased a friendly zephyr to the eastward. At sunrise we were alone on the sea, ghosting along at two knots.

11

A HALFHEARTED GROWL FROM THE ENGINE was the response when I pressed the starter button. The cause of the problem was immediately evident when I examined the batteries. A cell in the starting battery that we had replaced two weeks earlier in La Paz was completely dry. The acid was sloshing around in the bottom of the fiberglass battery box.

During the latter part of our sojourn in the Sea of Cortez, one of our two batteries had developed an insatiable lust for amperes. After acquiring as many amps as it possibly could, it would rapidly divest itself of them while doing very little productive work in the process. By the time we had reached La Paz, it had degenerated into a worthless, amp-devouring black hole. We had walked the streets of La Paz in search of a replacement.

There are two factors that make solving almost any kind of problem in Mexico difficult. One is the mañana syndrome discussed earlier, and the other, a similar one, is an attitude of congenial indifference to a customer's problem that appears to be woven into the fabric of business in Mexico.

When conducting business there, it is wise to remember that the fellow behind the counter, whom you are expecting to get highly involved with your battery problem, is quite possibly the same fellow who has thought nothing of parking his car on an incline for the last 10 months, in order to roll start it, so that he can avoid his own dead-battery problem.

Having spent most of the day and all of my patience locating and purchasing a new battery, I lugged it down a dirt road in the blazing afternoon sun. Dripping with perspiration, I stopped to rest for a moment. I propped the heavy battery on a ledge of a rock wall while Molly assured me that having a reliable battery for the passage to Panama would be well worth all of the effort. In a careless moment, while listening to her comforting words, I let the battery slip from my grasp. It fell about three feet, hitting a sharp outcropping of rock with an ominous thud. I believe I can remember my exact words as I stared down in disbelief at the battery lying on its side in the dirt: "Oh goodness me Molly, just see what I have done. I dropped our new battery and probably knocked all of the plates loose—what a pity." I *think* those were my exact words.

Before installing the battery, I had set it on a piece of cardboard in the cockpit overnight to check for acid leaks. None was evident at the time. Apparently the heat that was created while charging the battery, or the motion of the sea, had opened a hairline crack in the casing.

This was no way to begin a passage. I switched to the other battery, started the iron spinnaker, and set a course for Acapulco, 190 miles to the east-southeast.

We were paying for my sins. I had flagrantly transgressed against my time-proven master plan for peaceful coexistence with marine batteries.

None of the 12-volt batteries that served aboard *Swan* during our first few years of cruising came even remotely close to surviving until their stated warranty expiration dates. The average useful life of these batteries was just over two years. A warranty is of little consequence anyway if the battery chooses to expire when one is thousands of miles from a place where it can be exchanged; except that the warranty's implication of favorable longevity always fanned the flames of optimism that I felt each time I installed a commercial-grade, deep-cycle, heavy-duty, eternally loyal marine battery.

Over the years I have listened with rapt attention to knowledgeable people explain the dire consequences of sulfating battery plates. I have always felt chastened during these discussions because in my heart I knew that I had somehow contributed to our abysmal record with batteries; and I also knew, with absolute certainty, that the plates were sulfating even as we spoke.

However, I found that we were not alone in the cruising world with this problem. And because no one likes to finish last in anything, I have always been secretly buoyed up by someone's sad tale of a marine battery going belly-up not long after it was purchased. Having dealt with this exasperating problem for such a long time, I know exactly what the person is going through. This intimate knowledge has enabled me to mask my true feelings with appropriate compassionate remarks and sympathetic facial expressions.

Shortly after our circumnavigation I stumbled onto a solu tion to the problem— at least for us. I arbitrarily bestowed a maximum working life expectancy of two years on all 12-volt batteries, regardless of the glowing claims by the manufacturer.

At 12-month intervals the older of our two batteries was replaced without consideration of the state of its health. This way a battery was never on board for more than 24 months, and there was always one battery in its first year of service, the honeymoon period of marine batteries.

It was simply a question of adjusting the way we perceived batteries. We stopped regarding them as boat equipment and placed them in the category of expendable items, like oil filters. The result of this scheduled battery replacement system was eight years of failure-free electrical power.

Had I not deviated from the replacement schedule, I believe that peace and harmony might have reigned forever in the battery box. The battery that died in Baja had been scheduled to be mustered out of service when we were in San Diego. The battery carried a five-year warranty and looked like it had just been removed from the shipping carton—all black and shiny with a large, iridescent green lightning bolt emblazoned diagonally across the side beneath the 60-month warranty sticker. I am embarrassed to admit how easily I was seduced into abandoning my tried-and-true battery replacement system by the glitzy packaging and the implied promise of the warranty.

As I said, we were paying the price for my sins. But having to sail to Acapulco to spend a few days doing penance seemed like a price we could afford. We sailed in light airs under the protection of the sailing awning during the day, and motor-sailed in the relative cool of the evening. With only one functioning battery, we felt it was prudent to keep it in a fully charged state by running the engine after sundown during the high-amperage draw period.

The exhilaration of sailing into Acapulco Bay was dampened only slightly by the thought of facing another battery buying ordeal. From seaward, it appeared as if there wasn't a square foot of undeveloped land remaining anywhere one looked. We sailed around the perimeter of the bay on a sightseeing tour of the hotels and anchored in front of the Acapulco Yacht Club.

We launched the dinghy and I rowed ashore to the club to get directions to the Port Captain's office, leaving Molly on board the boat with the Q flag flying as a procedural precaution. The government offices were not open on Saturday, I was told, so the clearing-in business would have to wait until Monday. I walked across the street to a bustling service station, hoping to get a lead on where I could obtain a battery. I approached three young men who were seated on chairs that were tilted back on two legs, resting against the shady side of the building.

"Pardon me," I said, "do you know where I can buy a battery for my boat?" Three blank stares. I then said, "Comprende English?" Three heads shook no. Speaking in my best Pidgin-Spanish/caveman dialect I said, "Yate batteria no bueno—me want new." They responded to this jewel of communication by rocking forward in their chairs and talking animatedly among themselves. The result of this conference was three shoulder shrugs.

From behind me came a Spanish-accented woman's voice, "Can I help you, Señor?" I turned to see a well-dressed woman about 40 years of age standing beside her automobile. I explained the battery problem to her and asked her if the banks were open, as I needed to cash a traveler's check. They were not, but she offered to take me to a tourist money-exchange office near the hotels, and then to an automobile parts store that sold batteries. I was concerned that Molly would be worried, but this was too fortunate an opportunity to pass up. We drove to a nearby school to pick up her two daughters before heading across town.

This charming lady was a wonderful exception to the attitude of indifference in Mexico that I spoke of earlier. She oversaw the money exchange transaction and served as translator when I purchased the battery. The yacht club was out of her way so I insisted on taking a taxi for the return trip. She hailed a cab for me, established the price with the driver, and admonished me not to pay him one additional cent.

Taking her hand with both of my hands I said, "You are a sweetheart." Her puzzled look told me that she didn't understand. "You are an angel," I then said. Her smile told me she understood that.

Separating a tourist from his money has been developed into an art form in Acapulco. In addition to the restaurants, night clubs, and dinner cruises, shops selling all manner of merchandise line the streets and boulevards.

While I have always felt extremely fortunate that Molly would rather browse through a well-stocked hardware store than most any type of boutique, there is a negative side. She points out tools and items that she thinks I ought to have, which is like pushing drugs at an addict.

Between shopping at a huge government food store and two visits to a hardware store, we spent five weeks of our cruising budget during the five days we were in Acapulco. However, it all balanced out, because we would be six weeks working our way southward to the Panama Canal, with very few places to spend money en route.

To make the 3800-nautical-mile passage from the mouth of the Columbia River to the Panama Canal one must cross 38 degrees of latitude and 45 degrees of longitude. The latitude seemed about right; it was the 45 degrees of longitude that gave me a problem. That much easting (one eighth of a circumnavigation) didn't quite fit the mental map of North America that I carried in my mind.

Also, the fact that the course from Acapulco to Panama is

more easterly than southerly required some adjustment in my mind-set.

If it were possible to sail a direct route north from the Atlantic entrance of the Panama Canal, which is exactly at longitude 79°55ʹW, you would skim past Florida on the *eastern* side and come ashore at Charleston, South Carolina.

If, perchance, the reader's mental map is also in need of some minor adjustments, we will pause here for a moment to examine charts and globes.

I laid out the sailing track from Acapulco: 130 degrees true, to intersect a point 13°N, 95°W, then to a course of 115 degrees, which would stand us approximately 200 miles offshore as we crossed the treacherous Gulf of Tehuantepec.

Winds caused by continental highs moving south from the United States across the Gulf of Mexico are constricted and accelerated as they move through the narrow Tehuantepec mountain pass and rush violently down to the gulf, spreading out to sea and creating the dreaded "Tehuantepecer." When the wind is out of the north and the Texas AM radio stations are coming in loud and clear—watch out!

We opted for an offshore passage with the possibility of encountering heavy weather in open seas, rather than face the tedium and inherent risk of sneaking along, day and night, for hundreds of miles near the hazards of the shore, where the small fetch eliminates the threat of large seas but the winds can be ferocious. On the open-sea passage, the odds were against us slipping across the gulf between storms; but *Swan* wasn't, after all, an untried filly.

A fresh breeze swept across Acapulco Bay, driving *Swan* seaward under the main and jib on the starboard tack. It had been a good stop, as unscheduled stops often are, and we were reluctant to leave. The dour predictions in the sailing directions and our previous experience in Central American waters did nothing to allay these feelings. *Ocean Passages For The World* advised that bedeviling currents, unpredictable winds, and dead calms plagued this coastal region all the way to Panama.

The wind held through the night, and at sunrise the horizon was clear. We would not see land again for 20 days, during which time we sailed only 1260 miles for an average speed of just over two and a half knots.

At 1400 on the fifth day—375 struggling, sail-slatting miles later—we reached the course-change waypoint. Later, we would refer to the first leg of the passage as the "fast run."

As the sun set, the wind shifted to the north. Ominous black clouds scudded swiftly overhead. Sure enough—country music from an El Paso AM radio station boomed in as if we were in the next county. In the building wind we dropped the mainsail and ran up the storm trysail—"Tehuantepecer" or not, it was wind!

We continued to sail on a beam reach for three hours, then eased the sheets and fell off to seaward, putting the wind and waves two points abaft the beam.

Swan sailed at seven-plus knots through the rough seas on this black Pacific night. I lay awake in the bunk listening to the sounds of a sailing vessel running before a gale; the rush of the water; the occasional slam of a rogue sea against the hull; always exciting, and often, for me, the cause of insomnia. After an hour I gave up my attempt at sleeping and relieved Molly. There was no sense in both of us being awake.

It was a bumpy night of fitful dozing in a corner of the cockpit with an alarm set at half-hour intervals. Near dawn I became concerned by the size of the seas. I furled the storm trysail, slowing the boatspeed to five knots; a reduction in speed that had a calming effect on the boat's action, and me.

The double sailtrack on the mast made handling the storm trysail a simple matter. A single sail track requires the use of a track switch, and the sail slides are subject to binding at the switch. Of necessity, the switch must be located above the head of the mainsail in its furled position. On most sailboats this would be an awkward height at which to feed the heavy sail onto the main track if binding occurs, even in fair weather, and potentially dangerous in storm conditions.

Swan's separate trysail track extended downward to a comfortable waist height for hanking on the sail. The slides could be fed onto the track with one hand from a kneeling or crouching position while the sail was raised with the other hand, using a wire-halyard winch that did not require tailing.

Before I installed a piece of equipment during the building years, I asked myself this question: "How will this thing work when we are in a full-blown gale in the middle of the night, clawing off a lee shore in a violent seaway, seasick, with my hands numb from the freezing rain?" (Notice that I said this to myself, because in those days I was still in the process of convincing Molly how wonderful it was all going to be.)

Molly cooked a breakfast of our rough-weather standby: ramen noodles and crackers. With the mate in charge of the way of the ship, I fell asleep almost immediately after I finished eating. When I awoke three hours later, the wind had died almost completely and we were wallowing in the sloppy seas. It had been a rough ride, but we had outrun the perils of the Tehuantepec.

Eleven days into the passage, 720 miles out of Acapulco, *Swan* crept along in a faint breeze flying the doldrums rig. Vane's reactions were slow. His sluggish commands steered the boat through a 40-degree swing of the compass, but he was averaging the course.

Vane was performing his duties more reliably than his buddy CN. The satellite fixes had been erratic for the past month. A completely wild fix would occasionally occur within a series of accurate positions. I had verified this anomaly with celestial observations and bearings taken on the land.

While we were anchored at Socorro, CN blithely presented us with a fix that plunked us down, high and dry, a few miles north of Rangoon, Burma. Far-out positions like that were not a problem. Our concern was with fixes that might be in error, but still plausible enough to be believed. I decided to navigate as though we didn't have a satellite navigation set on board. The electronic fixes served only as a verification of the celestially obtained positions. My appreciation of the infinite reliability of the celestial bodies deepened.

At midday on December 9, 1990, I crossed a 1040 LOP of the sun with a noon latitude. I didn't bother advancing the line of position from the earlier sight—at a speed of just under one knot it would be stretching the term "running fix." I logged the results of the noon-to-noon run: a whopping 28 miles!

Suddenly the tranquility was shattered by a large bull dorado bursting through the placid surface of the sea. The iridescent lure flashed through the water as the fish made a deep dive, setting the hook and sealing its fate. We were surprised that the fish had hit the lure, as *Swan* was barely moving. Molly started the engine and we motored at three knots to keep tension on the line.

The dorado fouled the other trolling line when it streaked toward the boat. Then it made a powerful leap across the self-steering rudder, collided with the transom, and dove straight down. I pulled on the tangle of lines, drawing the fish in close to the boat. After several attempts, Molly gaffed the twisting, fighting fish, and with one great heave we slid the critter over the pushpit into the cockpit.

I held the enormous fish down on the cockpit seat. With a sudden twist of its body it freed itself from my grasp and leaped from the seat like an uncoiling spring. The blunt head shook violently, splattering us and the cockpit with blood. I threw a towel over the slippery fish and held its head down securely. In a last effort to escape, it lashed out with its tail, striking a powerful blow to Molly's leg. Finally, I pinned the struggling creature to the cockpit sole.

I looked up and was shocked to see a ship approaching less than a half mile on the starboard bow. We were in the heart of the San Francisco/Panama shipping lanes, but this was the first ship that we had seen since leaving Acapulco. We were not on a collision course, but it was disturbing that a ship had gotten that close without us seeing it.

The mate took charge of the situation and poured half a shot of vodka into the fish's gill. It died almost instantly. We had recently learned of this method of administering the *coup de grâce* to a dorado. It isn't effective on all species of fish.

I surveyed the surrounding scene: here were two people who had sailed tens of thousands of miles, with years and years of cruising experience, sailing their boat on a zigzag course at

141

less than a knot; covered with blood and standing in a tangled mass of fish lines, with Molly nearly in tears from the wallop the fish gave her; a ship bearing down on us, and a five-foot dorado lying in the cockpit drinking martinis.

The fish was a prize! It measured 57 inches in length; the largest dorado we had ever caught. The question was what to do with it.

Dorado does not freeze very well. When thawed, it becomes slightly mushy and some flavor is lost. However, it keeps very well refrigerated at a near freezing temperature. In fact, unlike most seafood, the flavor of dorado is enhanced after a day or two on ice.

Drying the fish is another alternative. The texture of the meat lends itself very well to drying, and if done properly it makes a delicious jerky and can be stored unrefrigerated. This is what we decided to do with the bulk of the fish.

I boned the dorado into four long fillets. One was put on ice to be cooked fresh, and the remainder were prepared for drying.

The fillets were cut into six-inch pieces; a length that fits nicely into a three-pound coffee can. Each fillet was sliced lengthwise into thin strips, like bacon, and marinated overnight in the refrigerator in a mixture of one part soy sauce, one part water, and a sprinkling of grated ginger.

To conserve soy sauce, the strips of fish were packed fairly tightly into the plastic jars containing the marinade.

The sailing conditions were about as poor as they get, but they were excellent for drying fish. *Swan* plugged along in a light breeze under the relentless blaze of the tropical sun. Her cabintop was adorned with foil-lined trays of drying fish, and covered with mosquito netting. Our strong aversion to flies required that the fish be covered, although there was little chance of finding a stowaway fly on board.

There was, however, another reason for the netting. It partially concealed the drying fish from the inquisitive looks of five blue-footed boobies that had decided to adopt *Swan* as, most assuredly, *Swan* would never have adopted them. They stayed with us for more than a week, choosing the bow pulpit for their quarters. Their ridiculous antics and petty squabbling provided us with an ongoing source of entertainment.

The boobies seemed uninterested in the drying dorado. The soy sauce or ginger must have disguised the scent of the fish, because the boobies' apparent newfound respect for our property ran diametrically counter to their primordial instincts; and, from our possibly prejudiced viewpoint, was categorically unbelievable.

Before placing the fish in the sun to dry, we sprinkled black pepper generously on one side of the strips. After about three hours, while the fish was still moist, we turned the pieces over. If the strips are allowed to dry completely without being turned, they will stick like glue to the foil or pan.

Drying conditions were so ideal that the fish dried in one day, which was unusual. The consistency and flavor were superb.

Bass, trigger fish, and dorado were the only fish that we had personal experience drying, though it is our understanding that most white-meat fish can be dried successfully.

If serving trays are not part of the shipboard inventory, sheets of aluminum foil with the edges folded up can be taped to the deck or cockpit seats and used as a drying surface.

Swan had become a veritable food factory. Shredded cabbage and grated carrots were the principal ingredients of our salads when the lettuce and tomato supply ran out. This change in the menu was the signal to begin alfalfa farming.

We placed a tablespoon of alfalfa seeds in a quart fruit jar with a ring-type lid. A circular piece of bronze screen fit inside the threaded ring instead of the sealing lid (See Fig. 9). The screen cover made the twice daily freshwater rinsing of the seeds a simple matter.

Between rinses, the jar was kept in a dark locker and covered loosely with a towel to prevent the rapid evaporation of moisture. Darkness is critical to the sprouting of the seeds. They must be fooled into believing that they are growing under an inch of moist topsoil on an Iowa farm.

Care should be taken that water does not stand in the bottom of the jar. Sprouts do not flourish if immersed in water. They should be thoroughly rinsed and the water drained off, leaving the seeds in a moist state. The wet seeds tend to stick to the sides of the jar, which is fine.

Depending on the ambient temperature, the sprouts are ready to "harvest" in about three days. Alfalfa sprouts and chopped onions with a vinegar and oil dressing make a pretty good "three-weeks-out" salad.

Mung beans can be sprouted in the same manner as alfalfa seeds. Bean sprouts add a fresh and lively taste to canned oriental foods and stir-fry dishes. Also, they can be eaten as a salad.

There is a large shoal, navigable for small craft, about 90 miles off the shores of Costa Rica, called Guardian Bank. The heavy shipping traffic between the Panama Canal and the west coast of the United States and Mexico passes inside the bank. Canal traffic to and from Hawaii passes outside the bank. The shipping lanes encompass a V-shaped no-man's-land northwestward of the shoal. *Swan* and crew lived in this windless wasteland during the week prior to raising the blue-gray mountains of Costa Rica.

The absence of shipping and our snail's pace lessened the need for vigilant night watches. We stood them more as a matter of habit than necessity, taking short catnaps during the night with an alarm set.

On this leg of the passage we put together a five-day string of light-air, plodding miles that stands as a record of nonachievement in our cruising experience. The noon-to-noon logged miles were 26-36-47-50-46.

These runs included an hour or two of motoring each day to charge the systems and to catch fish—and did we catch fish! In one six-hour period of sailing and motoring we caught three jack crevalle, one barracuda, three skipjack, one yellowfin, and three dorado. Of the 11 fish, we kept the yellowfin, the two largest dorado for jerky, and one skipjack for sashimi. The freezer was stuffed with fish.

During this day of frenzied fishing, our resident blue-foots nearly went out of their one-track minds. While we were land-

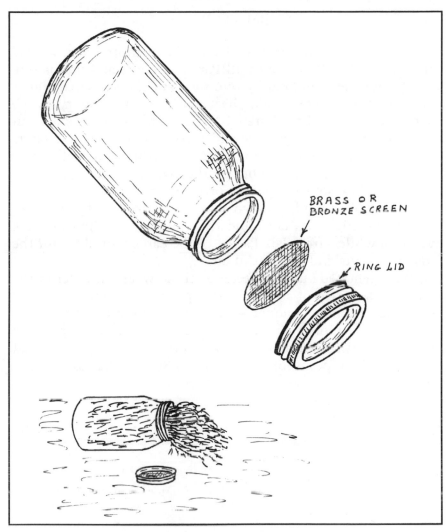

FIG. 9   *Fruit jar for sprouting alfalfa seeds and mung beans*

ing the fish, they flew around the boat screeching and squawking and colliding with the rigging.

I sighted land while making my way forward through the
trays of drying dorado to rotate the boobies. (Occasionally we
picked up the birds and pointed their business ends over the
side. They would then be sitting on the pulpit facing each other
in a semi-circle, which created the comical impression that
they were having a discussion.)

The sun was low in the sky as *Swan* motored in a dead calm toward Isla Parida, a small Panamanian island that is separated from the mainland by five miles of muddy shoal water. Aided only by a small-scale chart and a fuzzy memory of the cove where we had anchored 10 years earlier, we picked our way through a narrow passage and anchored in 30 feet of water.

To our great disappointment, the cascading waterfall where we had bathed and washed our clothes was nonexistent; probably rerouted by some tropical storm that had torn through the island. But this small letdown was overshadowed by the realization that night watches and the endless sail changes were over for a while—from Isla Parida to the canal would be, for the most part, an island-hopping affair.

We celebrated our often tedious three-week meander in the sun with a bottle of my specially produced "wine": spiked grape juice. Mellow bouquet—aggressive but not overbearing.

The mate took a sip of the grape and bestowed upon it a rather dubious compliment: "Well anyway, it's better than that stuff I paid 6000 pesos for at the Federal Store in La Paz."

AT ISLA SECAS, an island 20 miles ESE of Isla Parida, we rowed over to a Panamanian shrimp boat on the chance that they might be interested in trading shrimp for fish. They were. We traded two freshly caught skipjack tuna for six pounds of shrimp. The shrimp were a welcome change for us, as we were on the verge of sprouting gills.

No more than a hundred yards from where we were anchored, a lovely stream flowed down a slope that was covered with lush vegetation, and cascaded over the rocks into a crystal pool. The pool was about three feet deep and was naturally formed by sand and pebbles thrown up during periods of heavy surf. A small rivulet of sparkling water flowed from the pool over the beach to the sea.

After three weeks of water conservation, we reveled in the wonderful abundance of fresh water. One of my log entries says it best: "Most of the day was spent freaking out under the waterfall."

We filled *Swan*'s water tanks, washed our clothes, and rinsed off any remembrances left on the foredeck by our web-footed friends, who, after a 500-mile ocean cruise, grew tired of life in the anchorage and departed.

And so it went. We raised the anchor when the wind made up and sailed to the next island. If the wind failed to make an appearance, we stayed anchored for a day or two, or motored in the predawn coolness.

We had no schedule and only a rough itinerary. In this relaxed state of mind and body, the world that we knew to be real, seemed unreal. It was difficult to imagine that somewhere people were pushing and shoving their way aboard graffiti-covered subway trains, or trying to honk their way out of traffic jams.

Hector Alfredo Lòpez Romero was an unforgettable Panamanian. Among a host of other duties, such as delivering to the cook freshly killed chickens that just minutes earlier had been scratching and pecking the sunbaked earth, he managed the bar at an open-air restaurant which had a random collection of tables and a '50s-style jukebox that was never silent. Nearby was a row of claustrophobic rental cabins. The "resort" was located on a small bay, called Benao Cove, on the southern shore of Punta Mala at the western entrance to the Gulf of Panama.

The bay would be a dangerous place to anchor in southerly weather, but this was the season of northerlies. Even so, there was a constant surge in the bay that created breaking waves along the sandy beach. During our stay at Benao, the surf was small enough to make landing the dinghy possible, but large enough to make it sporting.

Hector was a young, unmarried, "can-do" fellow who spoke fluent English. No request was too great or too small. If it could be done, Hector would enthusiastically do it. When we learned that the nearest place to obtain diesel fuel was 20 mountainous miles away, Hector took charge of the problem. We left the jerry jugs at the pavilion in the morning, and in the evening they were magically filled with clean fuel at a modest charge.

I am certain that Hector was never more fervently devoted to assisting a cruising sailor than when a comely French singlehander, Francine, arrived. She sailed her sloop into the anchorage in a gentle breeze, wearing a few tiny bits of string and cloth for a bathing suit, while standing on the cockpit seat, steering with her toe.

Hector was moonstruck on the spot.

It was fortunate that our necessities had been taken care of earlier, because from that moment on it was almost impossible to get Hector's full attention, or even a fair portion of it. The

French lass, blonde and tanned, strolled on the beach like The Girl from Ipanema.

I chanced to meet her one morning while I was walking on the beach. She had sailed from France nearly two years earlier with tentative plans to circumnavigate. Her immediate sailing itinerary was flexible, and she was considering spending the cruising season in the Sea of Cortez before continuing to the westward. Being a neighborly sort of person, I offered to point out on the chart some good anchorages in the Panamanian islands that we had just visited, and our favorite places in the Sea of Cortez.

I saw Francine essentially as just another cruising sailor; a kindred soul as it were. It made little difference to me that she was young, svelte, sensuous, and extremely appealing. I would have regarded her in the same manner had she been homely as a mud fence and weighed 200 pounds. Character, intelligence, and ability were, of course, the traits that really mattered. This was, after all, the 1990s.

It was very quiet on board *Swan*, much too quiet, as I gathered up the charts in preparation to rowing over to Francine's boat. I asked Molly if she wanted to accompany me. She didn't. She was too busy.

About an hour later I returned to *Swan* to get the cruising guide for the Sea of Cortez. I explained to Molly that I had given Francine the chart of that area, and as the cruising guide would be of no further use to us, I was giving that to her also.

There was no immediate response from the mate, but as I was climbing into the dinghy she said, "While you're gone I think I'll make sure the galley sink is bolted down."

As I was rowing it occurred to me that perhaps my interpretation of the 1990s thing was a trifle simplistic; too black and white. It also occurred to me that Francine's route from France had probably left a turbulent trail of connubial discord in its wake.

But as Molly would be the first to agree, she was a cheerful, charming girl, and Hector's life was brightened immeasurably for a time.

When Francine sailed out of the bay, bound for Costa Rica,

Hector's world came crashing down. The chickens still pecked and scratched behind the pavilion, the jukebox still blared to high heaven, and the rum still flowed from his bar. But the void Francine left in the anchorage was no larger than the void in Hector's heart—his gossamer dreams had wafted away on the wings of the morning breeze.

With the working jib and storm trysail set, *Swan* emerged from the lee of Punta Mala into the teeth of a strong norther, close-reaching on the port tack, bound for Isla Pedro Gonzáles in the Perlas Islands, 65 miles to the northeast. The task at hand was to successfully traverse "Freighter Alley," a near-constant stream of ships heading for or departing from the Panama Canal. The lanes run north and south like a divided highway. At one point, while we were crossing the lanes, we counted nine ships.

In the small hours of the morning the wind slackened, and the rough seas subsided quickly with limited fetch to sustain them. We sailed on through the balmy night, moving out of harm's way.

The dawn brought with it a vague silhouette of an island fine on the port bow. Bearings taken on salient points verified it to be Gonzáles. Three hours later we sailed into the lee of the island and the wind died altogether.

Standing on the bow pulpit, I guided Molly with hand signals as we motored cautiously around a rocky outcropping and anchored in a protected nook near a small village.

The morning was hot and humid. Some women and young children from the village were wading in shallow water near the shore, and a few men and older children were diving off a gaudily painted, top-heavy boat anchored a short distance offshore. It was New Year's Eve and the men were getting an early start on the celebration—the rum bottle was uncorked.

We rowed over to where the men were swimming and introduced ourselves. We all shook hands and they offered us the rum bottle. Molly declined, which was appropriate, and I took a big swig, which was also appropriate, judging by the cheer from the men. They invited us to join them for the evening's festivities on the other side of the island. Transportation was not a problem—we would ride in style in the gaudy boat.

To escape the perils of the premature celebration we told them of our need to wash our clothes. They pointed to a stream running down the hillside which passed over some flat rocks that were perfect for pounding the clothing. I took a parting, fake drink from the jug and we rowed back to our boat to prepare for our date with the village "laundromat."

In the early evening the islanders came boisterously alongside. We frantically poked fenders between *Swan's* hull and the gaudy boat's rubrail, which was studded with protruding rusty nails. It was clear from the skipper's condition that the designated driver concept had not reached as far south as the Perlas Islands.

The two- or three-mile ride was a harrowing experience. The boat was overloaded, and at the slightest provocation it would begin to capsize. I was stationed on the cabintop with two teenaged boys who had not been imbibing. It was our job to thwart the boat's suicidal tendencies by quickly shifting our weight to the high side as the boat began to roll. The boys were adept at anticipating the direction of the next roll, and on two occasions their swift reactions probably prevented the boat from going to the bottom.

The skipper was very pleased with the performance of his human ballast, and he spent most of the trip entertaining Molly and the other women who were crowded into the tiny cabin. I was concerned about their ability to escape should the boat capsize.

We approached a hillside village on a small bay at a good clip in failing light, running blindly through the mooring buoys and sundry craft like the *Titanic* racing through the icebergs. At the last moment the skipper cut the power. I braced myself for the grounding as we glided toward the shore. I hardly felt it. The boat slid through the mud and came to rest in ankle-deep water on a falling tide. It was all planned. They didn't intend to use the boat for the return trip, and beaching it simplified the problem of disembarking.

I hadn't the foggiest idea how we were going to get back to

our boat after the party, but to my great relief it wasn't going to be in the gaudy boat.

An uneasy feeling of déjà vu crept over me as we made our way up the steep incline toward the village. We never liked leaving *Swan* anchored unattended in strange surroundings if we could not get back to her quickly. It was not only the capriciousness of the weather that we were concerned about. The passing of years had not erased from our memories the shock and anger we felt when we returned to the boat one evening in Costa Rica to find that she had been burglarized—radios ripped from their mountings, clothing and gear strewn everywhere. The scene was still vivid in our minds.

But we had decided long ago that one bad experience was not going to make us slaves to the boat. The long-distance cruising sailor always exists in a state of varying degrees of vulnerability—the ever-present threat of the elements; the occasional hostile port official; a failure of a vital piece of equipment or a serious medical emergency in a remote region. Risks such as these are intrinsic to the cruising life, but are part of the undiluted freedom and adventure, and the feeling of self-reliance that makes the life so unique and addictive.

The village was not what we expected to find. The houses shared common walls, with their fronts lining both sides of a hard-packed dirt lane 12 to 15 feet wide. Light shone through the open doorways, dimly illuminating the lane that was crowded with small groups of men laughing and talking, staring children, and barking dogs.

We entered a house that was essentially one large room with a curtained off area that was probably the bedroom. In the middle of the room was a large table with several men sitting around it drinking rum, some well into their cups. Two women were cooking at a large stove in a corner of the room. It was suffocatingly hot. A clear-glass light bulb with a blinding, white-hot filament, hung from the ceiling by a wire about three feet above the center of the table. Apparently the village had a communal power plant, though I couldn't hear it or anything else except loud rock music blaring from a gigantic boom box in the corner of the room.

"Buenas noches," we practically shouted as we sat down in the chairs offered us. "Buenas" echoed around the table as two small glasses of rum were set before us. We held the glasses up in a silent, nodding toast and downed the rum. The glasses were instantly refilled.

Presently, four cooked chickens were set on the table. The scrawny chicken on the platter in front of us appeared to have led a tough life. It looked like it might have hiked from Arkansas for the occasion. One of the men sliced off two skinny legs and handed them to us with a fork. We took a bite and uttered the old standby, "Bueno." Chicken was not just the main course, it was the only course.

For reasons known only to them, the women at the party asked Molly to accompany them to the house next door to model some of their dresses. She went with them and I stayed with the men, the chicken, and the rum.

It was an evening that remains foggy in my memory. Rum and greasy chicken, greasy chicken and rum, interspersed with sleight-of-hand tricks for the gaping children and an occasional pause to pass judgement on one of the dresses Molly was modeling; another two fingers of rum, and always the underlying concern of how we were going to get back to *Swan*.

The skipper of the gaudy boat had implied that transportation back to our boat wouldn't be a problem, but our experience with islanders everywhere was not to assume too much in the way of schedules. I hadn't seen the skipper for hours. Given the lengthy period that he had been celebrating, I suspected that he had found a comfortable bed under a palm tree somewhere.

By this time we were well into the new year. The filament seemed even brighter and the music louder—the faces around the table were fuzzy—I was definitely feeling the effects of the chicken.

Ten years earlier we had been in a similar situation on Contadora, an island in this same group. That evening had ended in a nightmarish nocturnal expedition through the jungle. Only this time we were farther from the boat, and I suspected that some rough terrain lay between us and the cove where *Swan* was anchored.

One of the men spoke English fairly well. I asked him about transportation back to the boat. He waved his hand in a sweeping, horizontal motion to seaward while shaking his head—the tide was out and all of the boats were sitting on the bottom. He made no suggestion that we stay the night, though the idea was not very appealing to me anyway.

I went next door to find Molly. She was wearing a black, slinky number that refreshed my memory about one of the reasons I had cajoled her into marrying me 18 years earlier. The women had been far more temperate than the men, but they were still a lively group. I told Molly that she might consider trading in the black dress for a "Jungle Jane" outfit. She looked at me quizzically. "Contadora," I said. "Oh . . . Contadora," she said.

I walked outside and made my way in the darkness to the edge of the village. The moonless sky was clear. I managed to find Polaris, which was a fair accomplishment considering that it is a second-magnitude star, that it was low in the sky, that my eyeglasses were on the boat, and, of course, that I'd had quite a bit of chicken. During the nerve-racking boat ride to the party I had managed to keep a vague accounting of the distance we had traveled, so I had a general idea of where we were on the island. According to my reckoning, *Swan* lay about two miles to the southeast behind a ridge of intimidating hills that were barely visible in the starlight.

I went back to the party, which was still raging. Chicken bones and empty bottles littered the table. I cornered the fellow who could speak English (slurred) and reiterated our transportation problem. He was an amiable sort and he assured me that he would handle the problem. Remarkably, he did. He left, then returned a few minutes later and said they were ready to go.

Molly and I followed a troop of men down the path to the beach. After much shouting, laughing, and what sounded like cursing, they hauled a narrow, blunt-bowed, nondescript wooden boat roughly 12 feet in length out of the brush. It was equipped with a large outboard engine. We dragged it through the tidal flat for perhaps 150 yards until we were in a sufficient depth of water to float the boat.

From unpleasant past experiences, we had long ago discarded our slip-on thongs of the type often worn by cruisers, because they are difficult to keep on your feet when wading and are dangerous when walking on slippery rocks. We were wearing deck shoes that served us well on this night, wading in water with a bottom covered with broken shells and who knew what. Molly's battered deck shoes, by the way, had been a comical accoutrement during her elegant fashion show.

Molly and I boarded the dinghy with the fellow who was going to drive the boat. Then, to our consternation, three of the men also got in to go along for the ride, grounding the boat in the shallows. We carried it out another 50 yards into hip-deep water and clambered back in.

Predictably, the driver only countenanced one speed: flat out. With such an overloaded boat there wasn't a ghost of a chance of getting up on a full plane, which wasn't a problem in the smooth waters of the bay. But when we rounded a promontory we were exposed to a fair chop, which was when the saltwater bath commenced. Molly and I occupied the bow area, serving as human breakwaters. The spray didn't seem to faze the driver or "crew," and there wasn't the slightest consideration given to the option of slowing down.

For about 20 interminable minutes we slammed our way around the island, clearing some of the outcroppings of rock by a few feet. We were in the tropics, but at four a.m., lightly clad, and running at 10 knots against the wind in a constant spray, the word is COLD! While our hosts were also lightly dressed, their liquid fortification had apparently rendered them immune to the chilling blast; also, they were receiving far less spray than we were. Molly, who has zero tolerance for even the suggestion of being cold, was shivering and shaking. I was in nearly the same state when, at last, I saw *Swan*'s anchor light. We chattered a "gracias" to our escort party as we climbed aboard *Swan*. They swung around in a tight circle, waved, and roared off into the darkness at full throttle.

We heated some fresh water and took one of the most pleasant and hottest cockpit showers that we could remember.

A faint light in the eastern sky heralded the dawn of the first day of the new year. We lay stretched out in our warm bunks while the boat rocked slowly in the gentle swell.

"Well I guess that wild ride was better than the Contadora jungle scene," Molly said.

"Definitely!" I answered. "You know," I said, raising myself up on one elbow, "I was just thinking how sexy you looked in that black dress. . . . "

"Go to sleep, Jim."

The morning sun rose above the tops of the palm trees clustered along the shore, sending shafts of light through the portholes. I was awakened with a start as *Swan* swung on her anchor and the brilliant sunlight played across my face.

I sat up quicker than my abused head could reasonably be expected to tolerate. The Comeuppance Department in my brain sent a sharp, painful message of displeasure to the Fun and Frolic Office (located between the temples) for authorizing such intemperance during the ushering in of 1991.

Caught in this bureaucratic crossfire, I gingerly got up and closed the porthole curtains, then swallowed three aspirins with two large glasses of iced tea and returned to the peaceful sanctuary of my bunk. I closed my eyes very slowly so they wouldn't make a loud click.

Our pre-party plan for this day had been to sail to an island a few miles north of Pedro Gonzáles to do some beachcombing; a plan of action that now had little chance of happening. There are days when anchors are best left undisturbed in the sand.

What seemed like only a few minutes later, although two hours had passed, I was awakened by the smell of perking coffee and the sound of an outboard motor in the distance. I felt far better than I had the right to feel, and Molly was chipper as usual.

The sound of the engine grew louder. We went on deck and were surprised to see the gaudy boat approaching. It appeared even more garish in the noonday sun.

It was a subdued group that came alongside. One of the

chief revelers at the party was lying on a thwart holding his head with both hands in an effort to shut out the world.

One man, two women, and the two mobile ballast boys came on board with a gift of a large stalk of bananas and a basket of coconuts.

Molly popped popcorn and served glasses of Tang, one of which was handed down to the indisposed man in the gaudy boat, along with two aspirins and a healthy dose of needling from his friends. Why the prostrate fellow would elect to go for a boat ride in the hot sun in his condition was a mystery to me.

They looked through our photo albums and we gave them a tour of the boat. As they were leaving, Molly gave each of the women a delicate shell necklace from Fiji. There was a simple and genuine goodness about these people of the Perlas Islands.

Early the next morning we motored out of the cove into a brisk wind blowing out of the east-northeast. We scrapped the beachcombing idea and laid a course for Taboga, 35 miles northwest of Pedro Gonzáles, and five miles from the entrance to the Panama Canal.

Rarely does a sailor receive the favorable treatment by the wind and weather in the Gulf of Panama that we experienced on the run to Taboga: sunny skies with scattered clouds, low humidity, and a spanking breeze on the quarter.

Flying the reacher and the single-reefed mainsail we covered the 35 miles in 5 hours and 15 minutes. Vane steered 34 of the miles while we sat under the awning reading and enjoying the effortless sail. As a bonus we caught a small barracuda as we were bringing in the trolling lines.

This short, exhilarating run was possibly *Swan's* last sail in the Pacific. She had voyaged more than 27,000 nautical miles within the confines of that vast ocean, north and south of the Equator. We like to think that, having seen her prove her mettle, the Pacific sent her off to the Atlantic side with a flourish.

13

THE PREFERRED ANCHORAGE near the hotel at Taboga was jammed with boats. The only open space was in a tidal stream between a small island and the town. We put down two anchors streamed from the bow, one in each direction of the tidal flow, Bahamian style, to limit our swinging radius when the 16-foot tides ebbed and flowed.

We had entertained the idea of provisioning the boat and conducting the canal transit business via the ferry that ran the nine miles between the island and Balboa. But after considering the security problem of *Swan* and the dinghy, and the hassle of several round trips on the ferry, we opted to take our chances of finding a transient mooring at the Balboa Yacht Club.

Swan motored toward the canal in the churning wake of the early morning ferry to Balboa. As we approached the ship channel I called Flamenco Signal, the harbor control station on the Pacific side, on VHF radio Channel 16. I was impressed with the explicitness of the instructions we received from the traffic controller, which I reconstruct here from scribbled shorthand: "Proceed toward the canal staying outside the ship channel on the right-hand side. Pass near but to the right of the red buoys. There is sufficient depth well outside the channel for small craft. Continue until you reach Buoy 16. The Balboa Yacht Club will be on your right. Pick up a mooring if one is available, or temporarily anchor."

The controller made no reference to the marine terms "port" or "starboard" in his instructions. He used the words "right" and "right-hand." These words are unambiguous.

From the outset of our boating experience we used the words *right* or *left* when giving steering instructions. One learns these words as a child; they become firmly ingrained, and the correct response to them is automatic when they are spoken in an emergency situation.

Phrases like *go to starboard of it* or *leave it to starboard* sound similar and, of course, have opposite meanings. The ambiguous directive, "Pass to starboard" when meeting a vessel traveling in the opposite direction requires clarification in order to resolve the helmsman's dilemma: "Whose starboard?"

We used the terms *port* and *starboard* to indicate the relative bearing of something from our boat such as "a ship broad on the port bow," but never as a steering directive.

There were several vacant transient moorings on the outer row, about 100 yards from the ship channel where wakes from the passing ships would be substantial. We picked up the floating polypropylene line from the mooring that we judged (in the superficial way that one evaluates moorings of unknown integrity) to be in the best condition.

A fellow on *JoLiGa 2*, a sailboat on an adjacent mooring, waved a hello to us. Later on, he would keep us on the edge of our seats with a harrowing tale of a singlehander's worst nightmare.

From its outward appearance, the Balboa Yacht Club seemed to be earnestly attempting to live up to its reputation as "the worst yacht club in the world." We had a mental picture of the club from a decade earlier; a picture that bore only a basic resemblance to the club as we now found it.

It had slid downhill dramatically during those years. Paint was scaling off the clubhouse, and it was in a state of general disrepair. The piers and fuel dock were in an equally sorry condition. As we were soon to discover, the club's degeneration was, in a general way, a reflection of what had happened to the Panama Canal itself, and to the once immaculate and impeccably maintained buildings in what had been the Canal Zone.

The yacht club provided a launch service 24 hours a day; a hangover from its halcyon days, and a necessity, as there was no place provided to moor a dinghy ashore. With varying degrees of success, a short blast of a horn would summon the launch. The success rate increased somewhat as the launch driver became aware of our presence, and service was nurtured by an occasional dollar bill tucked into the driver's pocket.

The transient mooring fee was $12 per day, plus a one-time fee of $15 for "club privileges." There were no laundry facilities and the showers were out of order, but one could feel free to step inside out of the rain.

A disclaimer on the registration form that I was required to sign did little to bolster my confidence in the integrity of the club's transient moorings: "The Balboa Yacht Club shall not become financially liable in any instance of mooring failure and any resulting financial cost from a mooring failure must be assumed by the boatowners involved."

It was like a passenger being financially responsible for the flat tire on the taxi he hired. But the yacht club was the only show in town and it served our purpose, in its fashion.

The baffling clearing-in procedure was simplified immeasurably with the assistance of Luis, a Panamanian taxi driver to whom we were introduced by an American couple who were also making the canal transit. Luis was honest and knew all of the legitimate shortcuts. For a very reasonable fee of $8 per hour, he and his little red Toyota were available. He accompanied us inside each office that we visited. He knew nearly everyone by name, and eased us through the bureaucratic maze.

In a time span of 1 hour and 45 minutes we had checked in with the Port Captain, where we were issued our cruising permit; cleared customs, obtained our visas at the immigration office, and arrived back at the club.

During the ride back to the club Luis pointed out the Canal Commission offices that we would need to visit to arrange our canal transit and pay our fees. He also gave us some straight information about hiring the Panamanian line-handlers that flocked to the yacht club on Tuesdays and Thursdays, the yacht transit days. His entrepreneurial spirit and positive attitude reminded us of Hector Romero in his pre-Francine days. Luis relied on word-of-mouth advertising, and, as one might expect after seeing him in action, he was seldom idle.

Panama City is a short distance from the Balboa Yacht Club, but required a taxi ride because of the risk of being robbed. Unemployment was disastrously high in this large modern city, and was a root cause of the crime problem. As bad as the lawlessness was, it paled in comparison to the rampant crime that plagued Colón, on the Atlantic side, and Panama City offered a wide range of products and services. Provisioning and other requirements of a cruising yacht, and the personal needs of its crew, were best taken care of here.

We spent most of one day shopping at the El Dorado Shopping Center on the outskirts of the city. A large supermarket in the complex carried a wide variety of American and Panamanian foods. If we followed our sailing itinerary, it would be our last major provisioning stop before we reached the United States.

The Balboa Yacht Club is located on Fort Amador. Certain taxis had clearances to drive on the post and others did not. Therefore, before hiring a taxi for the return trip, we questioned the driver to see if he had the necessary permit. The first two taxis we hailed did not; the third one did. Had we not checked, we would have been standing on the sidewalk at the post gate surrounded by bags and boxes of groceries. We had Luis to thank for our preparedness.

That evening we invited John Sloboda, the fellow on *JoLiGa 2*, on board for a drink. After hearing his story I pronounced him "the luckiest man on earth." He agreed completely.

John was sailing singlehanded to Balboa from the Perlas Islands with a nonfunctional auxiliary engine. When the evening breeze faltered and *JoLiGa 2* slowed to about two knots, John lashed the outboard-powered dinghy to the port quarter to serve as a tug.

Wearing only a T-shirt and carrying a flashlight, he climbed into the dinghy to fill the outboard motor's gasoline tank, while the boat sailed along in the gathering darkness on autopilot in a two-foot chop.

Suddenly, a small wave hit the dinghy. In an instant John found himself in the water watching his boat sail away without him! In a state of sheer panic he swam after his boat, unaware that he was still holding the flashlight, which greatly impeded his progress. The distance slowly widened between John and *JoLiGa 2* as he became exhausted from his desperate effort. But horrified at the thought of his probable fate, he continued to swim like a robot in the direction of his disappearing boat.

At approximately 2100, after three hours in the water, he saw what appeared to be the lights of an island about half a mile away. But there wasn't an island for 10 miles in any direction. It was a cruise ship!

With renewed spirit he swam toward the ship while screaming, "Help! Help! Mayday!" at the top of his lungs. Incredibly, someone heard him and the ship stopped and began sweeping the area with searchlights. Seeing nothing, the ship began to move away with the lights still playing across the water. John then set an unofficial decibel record for screaming at cruise ships and running on water. The ship stopped again. A searchlight found him. He was saved!

Within minutes the *M.S. Polaris* had put a ship's boat over the side and two men had yanked John out of the water.

As the boat came alongside the ship the passengers leaned over the railings with flashbulbs popping, while John lay happily and thankfully in the bottom of the boat in his T-shirt.

The watch on the bridge had seen John's boat sail by. The ship's captain dispatched the tender to retrieve the wandering *JoLiGa 2*, and called for a Panama Canal Pilot Boat. Sporting a *M.S. Polaris* T-shirt and shorts, a very grateful John Sloboda was taken to Balboa with his independent boat in tow.

It was an incredible story and certainly a strong case for wearing a safety harness at sea.

The situation in which we found ourselves that evening was unique to say the least: we were sitting in the cockpit of our boat on a waterway that divided two continents, moored in front of the worst yacht club in the world, listening to a story told to us by the luckiest man on earth!

We were pleasantly surprised when *Swan's* 1980 canal transit records popped up on the computer screen at the Canal

Commission Admeasurer's office. This saved us the time and bother of having the boat measured, plus the $60 charged for this procedure. The measurements are used to calculate the transit fee.

With our official business completed, all that remained to do was hire three line-handlers. The canal authorities require a transiting yacht to have four line-handlers on board in addition to the helmsman, regardless of the method used to negotiate the locks.

If a yacht side-ties to a tug, as we did on this transit, two line-handlers are sufficient and two go along for the ride. But four line-handlers are needed if the vessel "center-locks," which means that the boat is held securely in the center of the lock by four 100-foot lines running from the bow and stern cleats, port and starboard, to bollards atop the lock walls.

When center-locking, monkey fists attached to light messenger lines are heaved from four directions by men who "walk" the boat through the locks. The messenger lines are fastened to the 100-foot mooring lines and are hauled up to the bollards. As the lock fills or empties, the lines are taken in or payed out accordingly by the line-handlers on board the vessel.

Occasionally I have heard cruising sailors grumble about some of the rules that must be followed during a yacht's transit of the canal. These rules were developed during three quarters of a century of canal operation, and there are sound reasons for them, although they are not always readily apparent. Yachts are, and always have been, a money-losing nuisance for the canal. The $20 fee that we were charged for the transit, based on *Swan*'s tonnage, did not pay the costs of one hour of our pilot's time, and he spent a total of 10 hours on board. Having to comply with a rule that is not to one's liking is a small price to pay for the services rendered to transiting yachts by the canal people.

There is another option for the skipper who feels that he cannot tolerate the rules and regulations. It involves a little jaunt around the Horn.

On our walk back to the club we saw buildings in the old Canal Zone that had been struck by stray bullets during the attempted coup against General Noriega over a year earlier. Ugly splotches of unpainted, sloppily repaired stucco marred their appearance.

The once-pristine homes with manicured lawns and well kept gardens along the palm-lined residential streets had given way to a depressing seediness. The sense of an end of an era was almost palpable.

The canal experience had been the closest thing to colonialism in American history. Labels aside, it hadn't been all that bad for Panama. In fact, Panama would probably still be part of Colombia had it not been for Teddy Roosevelt using gunboat diplomacy to support Panama's declaration of independence. His iron will and penchant for using the presidency as a bully pulpit to advance his plans and policies were legendary. T.R. made things happen!

It is true, however, that viewed from today's perspective, some of his actions are open to criticism. He didn't exactly use kid gloves in the canal treaty negotiations with the fledgling Republic of Panama; and he killed off one hell of a bunch of animals on his hunting safaris in Africa. Still, sometimes in a wistful moment I long for the return of a "'Teddy."

We hired three Panamanian line-handlers for $45 each for one day's work. If the transit took two days, as it did, the second day's wage was $10 as it involved only a short period of locking down through the Gatun Locks on the Atlantic side. The three men spoke English fairly well, which made everything simpler.

If for any reason a yacht was not prepared to move at the appointed time of transit, the skipper was subject to a fine, reportedly $100. Also, the line-handlers would have to be compensated for their time. Because of this concern, I hired a fourth man for $10 dollars as a standby in case one of the line-handlers failed to appear.

On the transit day, all four of the men were at the dock very early in the morning. When I paid the standby fellow his $10, he waved the bill at the other three men and said with a big grin that was punctuated by a missing front tooth, "Easy money!"

MADDEN LAKE

MADDEN DAM

NAMA RAILROAD

RO
UEL
CKS

MIRAFLORES LAKE

TRANSISTHMIAN HIGHWAY

PANAMA CITY

MIRAFLORES LOCKS

PORT OF BALBOA

CANAL COMM. ADMIN. BLDG.

NTERAMERICAN HIGHWAY

HOWARD AIR FORCE BASE

BRIDGE OF AMERICAS

FOAT AMADOR

BALBOA YACHT CLUB

FLAMENCO

PACIFIC OCEAN

At 0915 we passed under the Bridge of the Americas, a connecting link of the Pan American Highway. The bridge was built at approximately the same location as the old ferry crossing that it replaced.

Our pilot was a cheerful veteran of 23 years of guiding vessels through the waterway. We learned a great deal from him about the operation of the canal, the detrimental effects of the slipshod maintenance the canal was receiving, and the future of the canal as he saw it.

We entered the lower Miraflores Lock in company with three other sailboats and a tug. Two of the yachts rafted together to center-lock, which is the preferable method for a yacht to negotiate the locks, in my opinion. We were instructed to tie alongside the tug, and the remaining boat, *Patience*, a yacht of Canadian registry, rafted alongside us. I reluctantly consented to side-tying after I was assured that the tug would not get under way until our lines were free, and we would move to the next lock under our own power. A skipper had a voice, albeit small, in the actual moving of the boat through the canal.

Part of my concern stemmed from an experience that we had had in Brazil during our first voyage. A tug that we were tied alongside had moved suddenly, bending three of *Swan*'s lifeline stanchions. I had avoided getting near a tug ever since.

The locking went smoothly and quickly. We motored across the small, man-made Miraflores Lake to the final ascending lock, Pedro Miguel. It was in this chamber during a short delay that we were able to see firsthand the deterioration of the locks: The huge gears and massive hinges that operate and support the lock gates were scaling with rust. The mitered edges of the gates were badly in need of servicing where they buttressed against the pressure of the dammed-up water. Large gouges and scrapes scarred the lock walls; damage that would have been repaired almost immediately when the American-run Panama Canal Company was in control, according to canal employees that I spoke with.

These seven-foot thick gates range from 47 to 82 feet high, and were built to a standard design. They are 65 feet wide and weigh from 400 to 700 tons. The lower portion of the gates are honeycombed with buoyancy chambers, and are so perfectly balanced that they can be opened or closed with a 40-horse-power electric motor in about two minutes.

The flotation chambers have another function besides delicately balancing the gates: They provide buoyancy when the gates are removed and taken to a dry dock for overhauling. Spare gates are hung immediately when this work is performed, thereby minimizing the interruption of canal traffic.

Even by today's standards the gates are a marvel of engineering. The design engineers seemed to have thought of everything, except how to ensure that their ingenious ideas would be utilized.

Clear of the Pedro Miguel locks, the four sailboats motored into the eight-mile long Gaillard Cut, named for Colonel David Gaillard, the engineer who was in charge of cutting through the Continental Divide.

Covered with mature vegetation, much of the sloping areas along the Gaillard Cut appeared almost as if the pass was naturally formed. But the scene before the canal project began, circa 1904, was a different story indeed.

I have a mental picture of the determined Colonel Gaillard sitting in a rowboat with his Chief Engineer, John F. Stevens, a railroad man. They are drifting somewhere near the spot where the Bridge of the Americas now stands, where the French had toiled for 20 years in an attempt to dig a sea-level canal. Faced with disease, a lack of funds, and flagging support at home, the French project had ended in abject failure.

Colonel Gaillard, who in my mental picture is the spitting image of the actor Alec Guinness playing the part of a no-nonsense English colonel, is undaunted by the French failure. He views the formidable barrier of rocky earth towering as high as a 30-story building as a worthy challenge. He can see ships passing through mountains.

Stevens is not so confident. "But sir, how will we ever be able to remove that mountain?"

"Trains, man, trains! We'll drill it, blast it, and dig it, and you'll haul it away in trains!"

Stevens considers leaping to his feet and saluting. But it's a small, tippy boat, and besides, he's not even in the Army.

Using pre-Model T Ford technology, the workers created a level bed 40 feet above sea level, digging through mountainous areas ranging as high as 280 feet above the canal bottom.

Plagued by bouts of malaria, the men blasted and dug through solid rock and shale in the tropical heat, rain, and mud, moving 200 trainloads a day of excavated material along an intricate network of tracks. The 200 million cubic yards of dirt and rock spoil were not just dumped. It was used to build dams, levees, and causeways. By any measure, this monumental effort was a triumph of engineering, and it stands today as an inspiring example of men prevailing against adversity.

From Gamboa, a community at the junction of the Chagres River and the Gaillard Cut, the canal follows the Chagres River bed, which lies far below the surface of what is now Gatun Lake.

In 1930, Madden Dam was built upstream of Gamboa to tame the wild and unpredictable Chagres. A large reservoir was thus formed, enabling engineers to maintain a relatively constant level of water in Gatun Lake. It also supplies hydroelectric power throughout Panama.

Once we were into the lake, Molly served lunch as we motored along the well-marked route at six knots. Our pilot had been in contact with Cristóbal Signal, the control station on the Atlantic side. He thought that we might have a chance of locking down in the late afternoon.

But it was not to be, even taking the three-mile shortcut through the old Banana Boat Channel that is used by small craft. The Gatun Lock gates were closing behind a freighter, our would-be locking companion, while we were still at binocular range.

It didn't really matter. The additional line-handler's wages were not much of a consideration, and we welcomed the prospect of swimming in fresh water. I was looking forward to diving under the boat to watch the eelgrass die on *Swan*'s thinning bottom paint.

A Canal Commission boat came alongside and picked up

our pilot. We then motored through the designated anchorage for 15 minutes looking for a shallow spot. Finally, with great reluctance, I dropped the anchor in 65 feet of water and ran out the entire 300 feet of anchor chain—a "first" in our cruising experience. I thought I felt a twinge in my back just letting the chain *out!*

With three strapping young men on board, I planned to get very busy checking the accuracy of the steering compass against my sextant observations of the emerging moons of Jupiter when it came time to bring in that spine-crunching mass of galvanized backache.

It turned out to be a great evening! After we all went over the side for a swim, which solved the bathing problem, I broke out my ukulele and a bottle of rum. Molly cooked a huge pot of spaghetti, choosing to keep the companionway door closed and endure the steamy heat of the galley while I twanged my uke for my captive audience.

To my surprise, they seemed to enjoy the music! I thought at first they were faking it to be polite, or maybe they believed that the dispensing of rum rations would continue as long as I kept playing; but I became convinced of their sincerity by their enthusiastic foot tapping and finger snapping to my jazzed-up rendition of *Just A Closer Walk With Thee.*

I was already painfully aware that Panamanians like rum and greasy chicken. I am now aware, but not painfully, that they also are very fond of rum and spaghetti.

In the morning we were informed by Cristóbal Signal on VHF radio that our scheduled transit time through the Gatun Locks was 1000. The time was subsequently changed to 1200, and then finally, at 1400, the four yachts locked down to the Atlantic Ocean, accompanied by a tug as before.

It is understandable that the yacht transit schedules are juggled in order to work them in with larger vessels as locking partners, because an average of 52 million gallons of Gatun Lake water are lost to the oceans with each complete ship transit of the canal. With a four-month dry season each year, water conservation is a constant concern.

Water usage during the locking operation has no direct correlation to transit fees. Four sailboats by themselves in a 110-foot-wide by 1000-foot-long lock are like toy boats in a bathtub, and displace very little water. Compare this to a Panamax (Panama Canal Maximum) vessel that is squeezed into the locks with "shoehorns and bear grease," and draws perhaps 35 feet of water. The Panamax vessel would use much less water than the four sailboats, yet it pays the highest transit tariffs.

A group of Pacific-bound yachts had departed from the Panama Canal Yacht Club that morning, leaving several transient slips open. *Swan* moored next to a Japanese couple who were cruising with their eight-year old daughter, Kurala, who could have been a finalist in the "Heart Stealer of All Time" contest.

In sharp contrast to nearly everything in the old Canal Zone, the yacht club had improved its facilities since we had last seen it. The mooring fee was a very reasonable nine dollars per day, with no charge for "club privileges." The showers worked and there was a clean and functioning laundry room. It was all very upbeat and well run, and I conveyed my positive sentiments to the club manager.

Without question, Colón was the most dangerous place we had ever been. Unemployment ranged at the 50-percent level, and crime had become a way of life for a desperate segment of the populace. The rampant crime had created a costly brigade of private guards and a disproportionately large police force, financed by the frightened citizens and business people in the city. Nearly every retail business, even the bakery, had an armed guard standing at the entrance. The doors and windows of nearly all of the business establishments were covered with steel bars. A policeman toting a rifle or submachine gun stood on most of the corners that we could see from the relative safety of the main street dividing Colón from the Port of Cristóbal.

We saw people cooking on open fires outside broken-down buildings and squalid shacks. Filth and litter were everywhere. It was an appalling place. History was in the process of repeating itself.

Colón was founded in 1852 during the construction of the

Panamanian Railroad that spanned the isthmus. The railroad was completed in time to provide a land link between sailing ships carrying men and material to and from the eastern United States and California during the gold rush. Colón flourished while the party lasted, then slowly declined into a shanty town by the end of the century.

In 1904 the town was revived by the beginning of the construction of the canal. It remained fairly prosperous from tourism and canal-generated revenues for most of the present century.

From all appearances, Colón is in the midst of a downhill slide that will most likely worsen as the American presence in Panama continues to diminish. Tourism suffered because of the uncertain political situation, the drug trafficking, and the absence of the security and stability that the American Canal Zone created. Before the Canal Zone was eliminated by treaty, Colón was a little piece of Panama, surrounded by what was essentially American soil with corridor access. Now is it surrounded by Panama. Colón has experienced one fortuitous bailout in its history, but I don't expect a rebirth for this pathetic city any time soon.

Fortunately, the crew of a yacht can complete the port clearance formalities without setting foot in Colón. The business is completed in the Port of Cristóbal, although the line of demarcation between the two places is not as sharply defined as it once was.

Harry Bryan, the builder and skipper of *Patience*, accompanied me on a daylight sortie to a vegetable market on the fringe of Colón to purchase fresh food for the passage through the Caribbean. I left my wallet on the boat and carried just enough money with me to make robbery affordable.

I enjoyed Harry's company for reasons other than security. He had a keen sense of humor, as did his wife Martha, and their teenaged daughter Sadie and son Warren. They had cruised through the South Pacific and were headed home to New Brunswick. They sailed on the following day. But unlike so many instances when cruising friends part company and never see one another again, we would have the pleasure of crossing their path as we meandered northward.

It was also time for us to go. We had mixed feelings about what lay before us: the promise of new adventure weighed against a windward slog through the Northeast Trades in the season of northerly gales.

This passage differed from our run out of the trades from Hawaii. On that windward passage, slipping to the westward only added miles to the voyage; leeway made to the west on this passage could place the boat in hazardous waters. The west-setting current working in concert with heavy tradewinds was capable of doing just that.

A course 10 degrees east of north had to be made good to safely clear the banks and reefs that were scattered over a large area west of the course line to our next intended landfall, Grand Cayman Island. Many of these low-lying hazards become visible about the same time that the roar of the surf can be heard breaking upon them. We had heard this terrifying sound one dark night off the northern coast of Australia when we found ourselves in shoal water as the result of a plotting error. It left an indelible mark on our memories.

With our port clearance in order we moved from the yacht club to the "flats," the designated anchorage for small craft. From this spot in the windswept harbor we could see large combers crashing on the Cristóbal breakwaters, sending spume flying high in the air. This display of unbridled power did not make the 600-mile passage to Grand Cayman seem any shorter.

The flats offer a comfortable spot to procrastinate for a day or so. It's a good place to watch one last B-movie and perhaps the "final round play on Sunday" on the Armed Forces Television station. It's a nice little shock absorber between life at the yacht club and green-seas-over-the-bow-time.

On the night before we left we stayed up until after midnight, sitting in the cockpit watching the ships moving slowly to and from Gatun Locks.

What would become of this place? Would Panama hire a private American company to take over the operation of the canal, as rumored? No one seemed to know.

The canal is truly a modern-day wonder; a tribute to American resourcefulness and ingenuity. It was completed ahead of schedule, under budget, and it was mandated by law to operate at no cost to the taxpayers and at no profit, thereby keeping transit costs to an absolute minimum. It operated according to this mandate for three quarters of a century. These days, it seems, any government project that shows signs of functioning that well is doomed. It's positively un-American!

In 1980, shortly after the canal treaty between the United States and Panama took effect, I observed, "for a fleeting moment I thought I heard Teddy Roosevelt turn over in his grave." Given the rate of decline that the canal has experienced since that time, it's just possible that in Heavenly Circles, T.R. might now be known as "Pinwheel Teddy."

14

"FALL IN BEHIND THAT BIG LOAD of trade deficit," I called to Molly, relaying my version of Cristóbal Signal's instructions for us to follow a Korean Panamax containership through the breakwaters. The ship looked like one of the World Trade Center buildings lying on its side. Containers were stacked five-high on the deck from one end of the ship to the other.

Beyond the breakwaters I went on deck to raise the mule team: the working jib and storm trysail. We were motoring about 100 yards behind the giant ship in a mass of swirling eddies in a dead- flat sea. About 30 yards on each side of us large rollers charged past. I had a momentary vision of *Swan* sailing snugly behind the ship like a pilot fish shadowing a great white shark, following the ship anywhere it went, so long as it was in a northerly direction. That pipe dream vanished when the bridge of the World Trade Center rang for more steam.

With the sails close-hauled on the starboard tack, the Vane pointing up on the verge of luffing, the compass read 345 degrees; fully 35 degrees to the westward of the sailing track I had laid out on the chart.

In this part of the Caribbean there is almost no magnetic variation. Magnetic headings do not have to be converted to true headings and vice-versa. The compass reads essentially true directions. North is north. Very convenient.

For an hour we bashed into the heavy ground swell to get a small offing, then changed to the port tack to take advantage of the countercurrent that sets eastward along the coast at about one knot. Every mile of easting would make the sail to Grand Cayman that much easier.

Three hours later, Portobelo, a small harbor 15 miles from Cristóbal was close abeam. On an impulse, I eased the sheets and we sailed into the lee of the seaward promontory of the snug little bay that opens to the west. It had been a hard day's work and we'd earned a well-deserved rest!

Once again we were being rudely reminded of a fact of our sailing life: As members of the informal fraternity of cruising sailors, we had never been very near the top of the list for notable achievements in the "Thrashing to Windward" category of cruising under sail. Actually, the evidence strongly suggested that we were pretty near the rear of the pack, and we didn't seem to be showing any signs of improvement in the initial stage of this passage.

This shortcoming was apparently fairly obvious to others early on in our cruising experience. In 1979, at a social gathering at the Point Yacht Club in Durban, a grossly insensitive acquaintance of ours explained to anyone within earshot his theory of the reason for our presence in South Africa. He said that *Swan* and crew had merely gotten so far downwind that to keep going west was the only reasonable alternative left to us.

I've always felt that this particularly vicious remark had the effect of watering down our circumnavigation. It bestowed upon us the dubious distinction of having sailed around the world unintentionally.

We stayed at Portobelo for two days. The anchorage was perfect and we had it all to ourselves.

The town was chock-full of history. Moss-covered ruins of a fortress built by Spanish conquistadors in the 16th century formed a bulwark in front of the small town. For two centuries Portobelo was the western terminus of the Spanish fleet of galleons that transported gold, silver, and other plundered treasures from South America back to Spain.

In 1668 the Welsh buccaneer, Henry Morgan, sacked the town. And in 1741 Admiral Vernon took the stronghold with six British men-of- war, pounding the fort into submission.

Our only brush with piracy and plunder while we were

there was when three small boys paddled out to *Swan* in a leaky boat that resembled a coffin. Two of the boys propelled the unwieldy box with short lengths of board while the third boy bailed furiously.

Molly appeased the black-hearted rogues with a handful of bubble gum each. With beaming smiles they paddled back to shore while the boy in charge of bailing threw water out of the floating sieve at a prodigious rate with one hand, and stuffed bubble gum in his mouth with the other.

In a light morning mist, under a gray sky, *Swan* beat along the coast. Once clear of the headland where the land bears away to the east, we eased off to follow the coast toward the San Blas Islands. Our tentative plan was to stop at this island group and wait for a favorable shift in the tradewinds.

We were pleasantly surprised in the late afternoon when the wind veered a point or two eastward. We hardened the sheets and brought the boat up full and by. The compass read 95 degrees.

Ready about! *Swan* came through the wind and we made off the land on a course just east of north. It was a delayed start, but not a bad one. We were 60 miles east of Cristóbal, sailing close to the desired course, and it would be at least a full day's sail before we entered the adverse, west-setting current.

Although CN had been performing very well for the past month, I still wasn't willing to bet the farm on him. I regarded him like a court witness caught perjuring himself. From that moment on the witness is presumed to be lying. As on the passage from Acapulco to Panama, I planned to navigate celestially, using the fixes produced by the perjurious CN for verification purposes only.

Weather permitting, I planned to take morning and evening star sights and a running fix of the sun each day until Serranilla Banks and Bajo Nuevo Banks, the northernmost hazards on this passage, lay astern.

Before leaving Cristóbal I had laid out the rhumbline on the chart and circled all proximate hazards in red. I had also circled the latitude and longitude lines where they intersected at five-degree intervals to help eliminate the potential for plotting errors caused by the profusion of Loran lines and shipping tracks on the chart.

This use of the red pencil had become part of our navigational procedure ever since I made the blunder of plotting a star fix from the east/west shipping track instead of a parallel of latitude in the Arafura Sea. The erroneous fix placed us 11 miles farther from shore than our actual position. Because of overcast conditions we had not been able to get a celestial fix for two days, and the false position seemed reasonably in line with my reckoning. As a result of that error, we heard the unexpected and frightening sound of breakers in the night that I spoke of in the previous chapter. Eye-catching red warning marks can save the ship when the fatigued navigator is having trouble focusing a tired mind and eyes on tiny marks on a chart.

Whenever depths on an ocean chart were indicated in meters rather than fathoms, I wrote the word "meters" in bold red letters at the top of the chart. Most of our small-scale ocean charts indicated sounding in fathoms and heights in feet, which had shaped our mind-set over the years. Fathoms and feet were automatic, meters were not. However, if one's charts and mind-set are in meters, then fathoms and feet should be treated as the foreign entity and indicated in bold red letters at the top of the chart. Warnings may be printed all over a chart, but the ones that the navigator has put there himself maintain their special importance, even when fatigue has dulled the mind.

These precautions may seem extreme to the well-rested student attending Navigation 101. But they do not seem excessive when you are hauling to windward in the fourth day of a full-blown gale, dead on your feet, and unable to sleep because of that worrisome labyrinth of coral to leeward and that dreadful knocking sound coming from the rudder.

On the evening of January 17, 1991, two days out and 215 miles north of Cristóbal, a Voice of America shortwave radio broadcast announced that United States-led air units had launched a series of air attacks against targets in Iraq. Our country was at war!

Such is the isolation of a boat at sea that one's thoughts are distilled down to the immediate concerns, and ours were certainly not about Saddam Hussein, although we solidly supported the President's actions. President Bush had a coalition of 28 countries to help him deal with Hussein, and there were just two of us to worry about Roncador Cay, a wreck-strewn reef 250 miles due north of Cristóbal. The reef lay 35 miles north-northwest of our DR position—it had our undivided attention as night descended. Current and leeway had been eroding our hard-earned easting. With every hour that passed we were being set closer to the reef. Force 6 winds had created steep-to-hard seas that would occasionally cause *Swan* to stall, exacerbating the leeway problem.

As the danger was not yet imminent, I decided to motor-sail rather than tack. The added drive created by the engine enabled *Swan* to punch through the seas, pointing up to an average course of 015 True; a course that if maintained, would see us safely past the reef unless I had underestimated the strength of the current.

It was a night of vigilance with very little sleep for either of us. CN was producing fixes that verified the DR positions, which was reassuring. He was making a sterling effort to regain his credibility.

At 0555, Beginning Morning Nautical Twilight, I woke Molly to help with the morning round of star sights. I have taken star sights unassisted many times, though it is much easier and usually more accurate when an assistant reads the chronometer and records the observed altitudes, especially in rough conditions like those we were experiencing.

Before continuing, I would suggest that those readers who would rather have a tooth drilled than read a word about celestial navigation, please flip forward a few pages until the dreaded thing is over. And should we ever meet, let me know that you skipped these pages and I'll spin a little yarn especially for you, just to make amends. I promise you it will be so salty and original that you'll swear I made it up!

When we conceived the idea to build a boat and sail it to the South Pacific, I knew that I must have a clear understanding of the principles of celestial navigation and be reasonably

181

proficient with the sextant for our dubious plan to have a chance of succeeding. At that point in my life I had never seen a sextant used, except in the movies.

I enrolled in a class on the subject, but quickly despaired of the snail's pace of instruction. It would have literally taken years to complete all of the peripheral courses that were required. I decided that I would teach myself. This was one of my better decisions.

I purchased a beginner's book on the subject. Thankfully, the author steered me in the right direction. He strongly recommended purchasing the three-volume set of *249 Sight Reduction Tables* that were published by the Hydrographic Office. I bought the set and I have never regretted this decision.

Within a month of home study (at work, at niece's ballet recitals, while driving on the freeway) it all began to make sense.

I had never been too concerned about my ability to learn how to use the sun to navigate. It was up there all alone shining at you. Pretty hard to miss. I knew where it was when I was two years old. It was the stars that had me buffaloed.

On a moonless night I had stood on an Oregon beach gazing up at that great star-studded dome above me thinking, "How will I ever learn all of this stuff? I'll never be able to identify and remember the names of the stars and constellations they're in."

Then I learned the good news. It wasn't necessary to memorize them! H.O. 249, Volume I, the tables for Selected Stars, does the identification for you! However, one does learn the names of many of these heavenly guideposts in the course of working with them.

The wizards who compiled the astronomical data for the tables arranged it in a consummately usable way. They didn't expect a scared farm boy from Kansas, flying in a flak-riddled bomber, choking on acrid smoke in the claustrophobic navigator's bubble, to be able to identify the left rear hoof of Pegasus.

It is not my intent to teach navigation here. Instead I want to present an overview of how this remarkably reliable means of navigating a ship at sea applies to a cruising yacht.

It is hardly necessary to explain the difference between peering at a celestial body through the scope of a sextant from the relatively stable bridge of a supertanker high above the waves, and doing the same thing from the heaving deck of a 36-foot sailboat that often disappears from view in the troughs of the sea.

Because *Swan* is being set toward the reef and Molly is standing at the companionway half asleep with clipboard in hand, I will be as brief as possible.

Volume I, H.O. 249, lists seven selected navigational stars for every degree of latitude from pole to pole. To determine the seven stars that will be used for a specific area on the earth, and the eventual position that will be obtained as a result of the observation of these stars, it is necessary to know the date, Greenwich Mean Time (G.M.T.), local time, and the rough position of the ship, which can be in error by many miles with little effect on the process.

The ability to add and subtract is the *only* mathematical requirement needed to reduce a celestial observation with a sextant to a fix on the chart. The wizards have performed the spherical trigonometry for you.

The question of when to take the sights is answered in the Twilight Tables in the Nautical Almanac for the specific date and the approximate latitude of the ship. To take a star sight there must be adequate light to make the horizon discernible, but not so much that the stars do not stand out sufficiently bright against the backdrop of the heavens. Therefore, observation time is limited.

As a general rule I observed the eastern stars first, both in the morning and evening. In the morning the eastern stars fade quickly in the lightening sky, and obfuscation of the eastern horizon is the primary concern in the evening as the sun sets. The western horizon is illuminated longer.

If all stars were uniformly bright and visibility was always 100 percent, this would be an inflexible rule. But as this is not the case, the observation sequence can be altered by cloudy conditions and the brightness or dimness of the stars being observed.

It is difficult to extol the virtues of Volume I too much. The approximate altitude of the body and its azimuth, or direction from the ship, can be determined beforehand by following some simple steps.

When it is time to take the sights, one merely presets the sextant at the altitude given for the particular star in Volume I as a result of the preliminary "stars work-up" that has been completed, and points it in the direction also given in the tables. Voilà! The star appears in the eyepiece near the horizon! The star will appear in the scope with a minimum of searching when one becomes proficient with the instrument.

This procedure should be practiced until it can be performed skillfully while standing on solid ground before attempting it on board a boat. The seas will not politely wait to hear a "Voilà!" before they slam into the hull, launching the preoccupied fledgling navigator in a soaring arc over the life-lines.

We learned this lesson the hard way. My initial plan had been to teach Molly how to use the sextant after I had mastered the necessary skills myself. This was to be done before we left on our voyage. In time, I became proficient in the use of the sextant, but with the myriad details to attend to in preparing to leave, I never found the time to teach Molly, other than giving the subject occasional lip service. I decided that I would teach her at sea, in direct violation of my rule that nothing should be learned at sea that could be learned beforehand in port.

Now I have been called many things in my life, but "patient" was never one of them. Suffice it to say that Molly eventually learned to use the sextant. But I would add that of all the problems real or imagined that we faced as greenhorn sailors, and the many and varied concerns that we had during that early period while I was teaching Molly to use the sextant at sea, birth control wasn't one of them.

The seven selected stars are chosen because they are *isolated* and make their appearance early in the evening, and linger in the morning twilight. Because of their isolation, a friend of ours who had no knowledge of the seven navigational stars, was able to pick out four of them during nautical twilight with no previous coaching other than being told that the stars were isolated.

I found that my most accurate sights were taken from a standing position in the center of the cockpit. This was as close to the longitudinal axis of the boat as I could get, thus minimizing the effects of the action of the sea. By flexing my legs as the boat rolled, I was able to cancel out or absorb much of the boat's movement. The objective was to "float" the sextant as if it were apart from the boat, with the degree of success of this effort dependent on the sea state. Leaning against the mast taking a sextant sight in the reddish glow of the setting sun makes great photographs and bad fixes.

Once the image of the star is near the horizon, the adjusting knob, called a micrometer knob, must be turned to raise or lower the body until it is superimposed on the horizon like a dot on a line. It must just "kiss" the horizon.

The sextant is then tilted slightly to the left and right. This causes the body to move in an arcing motion like a pendulum. Fine adjustments are made with the micrometer knob until the celestial body kisses the horizon at the bottom of the arc. This process ensures that the body and its reflected image are in exact vertical alignment when the altitude measurement is made.

At that precise moment, "mark" is called out by the observer and the assistant notes the exact moment of G.M.T., reading seconds first, then the minutes, and then the hour. The sextant altitude is also recorded.

Time, like a high-speed camera shutter stopping a bullet in flight, has frozen the position of the observed body in its relation to the rotating surface of the earth at the instant of the sight.

Exact time is critical to an accurate position derived from a celestial body. If the ship is sitting at the Equator and the body is directly overhead, its apparent motion caused by the rotation of the earth is 900 knots—15 miles per minute—a mile every four seconds. Quartz timepieces and WWV shortwave radio time signals make precise timekeeping a simple matter.

The Nautical Almanac and sight reduction tables are used

to reduce the sextant altitude measurement of the body and the G.M.T. of the sight to a line of position on the chart. Whether or not the ship is actually on that line depends on the accuracy of the time of the sight and the expertise of the observer. An error of one minute of arc, or 1/60th of a degree, equates to one nautical mile of error on the earth's surface. If one is able to fix the position of a yacht at sea within an error tolerance of one mile by means of celestial observations with a sextant, he, she, or it, is a member of a very select group. It can be done.

Reducing the results of a sextant observation of a celestial body to a line of position on a chart is a process of pure mathematics. Finessing the image of a celestial body down to the horizon with a sextant while standing on the deck of a rolling pitching boat is an acquired skill. A fix obtained from the observation of a celestial body is a unique mixture of an art and science. With a reasonable amount of effort put forth, this mixture can be mastered by anyone with average intelligence and a modicum of manual dexterity.

When that lightning bolt hits nearby and zaps all of the electronic systems on the boat, or some such calamity occurs when you are 500 miles from the nearest land, those celestial beacons whirling through the heavens won't let you down.

"Molly! *Molly!*" She had fallen asleep on her clipboard. Magically, it was still 0555.

To ease the motion while the star sights were taken, we fell off the wind 15 degrees.

Three of the seven selected stars, Vega, Rigil Kent, and Regulus, had asterisks by their names in Volume I, indicating that they were the stars whose azimuths were nearest the ideal 120-degree spacing between bodies for a three-star fix. Their azimuths were: Vega 053, Rigil Kent 171, and Regulus at 275 degrees.

I observed those three stars and took a backup sight of the planet Jupiter. The atmospheric conditions were fairly good for taking sights, except for the eastern horizon, which was partially obscured by a passing squall.

Before the coffee had finished perking, the three lines of position were plotted. Such is the remarkable utility of Volume I.

The lines of position formed a triangle that a three-mile diameter circle would have fit snugly inside. I marked the fix on the chart at the western part of the triangle near the point where the Regulus and Regil Kent lines of positions crossed, instead of in the center, because the accuracy of the Vega sight was in question. If I had the slightest doubt about the accuracy of a sight taken in the proximity of land, I felt it was prudent to err by placing the fix closer to the potential hazard as insurance (See Fig. 10).

To be fussy, I plotted the Jupiter sight, which passed nearly through the middle of the triangle. CN got into the act minutes later, verifying the verification.

The danger was clearly past. Roncador Cay would have to lie in wait for another vessel. The reef lay 15 miles to the west-northwest of our position.

In this discussion of navigation by the stars, I realize that I have ignored Volumes II and III. This is because I generally did not use them for star-sight reduction, although they can be used for certain stars whose declinations fall within the range of those tables. Those volumes are principally used to reduce sights taken of the sun, moon, and the navigational planets. If the weather conditions were such that I was unable to see at least two of the seven selected stars in Volume I, I usually didn't attempt to locate the stars covered in the other two volumes.

Volume I is like a sleek racehorse—fast and unencumbered. The other two volumes are more like draft horses, plodding through codes, declinations, and other minutia necessary to reduce a celestial sight. This is not to denigrate the volumes in any way. They are functional and well laid out, and, of necessity, are more involved with details which make them a bit tedious to use.

Volumes II and III contain data that is permanent in character and scope. Therefore, they never need to be updated. Volume I, like the racehorse, grows old. It must be replaced at

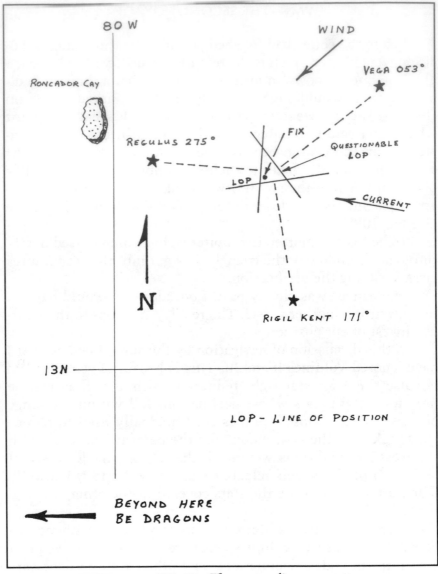

FIG. 10 *Three-star fix*

about five-year intervals, called epochs. This is because of scientific forces that eggheads understand, like "precession of the equinoxes" and "nutation," and other mysterious things you need not know to navigate your ship by the stars. However, it would be better all round if the universe were more stable. It is definitely something Washington should look into asap.

One last note. The Defense Mapping Agency now publishes the 249 tables and the prefix H.O. has been dropped. I used the prefix because it is how the tables are generally known.

Two things happened in the late afternoon that brightened our day. The wind made a small eastward shift with a decrease in strength, and we caught a 12-pound albacore.

For three days we had been catching floating seaweed that abounded in those waters. We had become so accustomed to hearing the snap of the clothes pin that alerted us to the seaweed "strikes" that we must have dragged the fish for miles. It was the only fish we caught on the passage.

We had been spoiled beyond redemption by the superb fishing in the Sea of Cortez. It ruined us for life. Normal fishing waters seemed like barren wastelands by comparison. The variety and plentifulness of the fish and sea life there exceeded anything we had seen anywhere in the world, including the Great Barrier Reef. All of the surface-feeding fish that we caught in that sea, and elsewhere, were caught with the same inexpensive trolling gear of the type that an old Hawaiian fisherman on the island of Molokai put together for me during our first year of cruising.

Our fishing underway had nothing to do with sport. When a fish hit the trolling line and was solidly hooked, it rarely got off. I think I can count the times that a fish got away on the fingers of one hand—well—maybe.

Only once did the gear break. Whatever it was that broke it, probably a shark, was so large that it merely saved us the trouble of cutting it loose!

The rubber squid lures that we used are known by many names. In Hawaii they were called "hoochies." They are sold in tackle shops and commercial fishing supply stores in a variety of sizes and colors. Seldom does one meet a hoochie-using fisherman who doesn't know the color that "really works!" Molly swears by pink.

We used a squid lure five inches in length with a galvanized or stainless-steel double hook about two and a half inches long. This combination caught fish from 40 pounds down to a sliver of a barracuda that managed somehow to get its mouth over one of the hooks.

A five-foot length of 90- to 110-pound test, stainless-steel flexible leader is swaged to the hook, using the appropriate size swages and crimping pliers designed for this purpose.

An oval-shaped lead weight is placed into the rubber squid's head with the leader wire passing through the hole in its center and the forward tip of the lure. The hook is then pulled tight against the lead, and the rubber "skirt" of the squid is trimmed so that about one inch of the skirt extends past the hook. If the skirt is left too long, a fish might get a taste of the phony squid without the sharp seasoning of the hook (See Fig. 11).

A small eye is swaged on the other end of the leader and attached to the trolling line by a spiral connector and a commercial-grade swivel.

After having done a great deal of experimenting with the length of the trolling lines, I'm not sure if length makes any difference. On this voyage we trailed two 5/32" diameter nylon trolling lines, one 80 feet and the other 85 feet in length with excellent results. We used larger line than was actually required, because it was easier on our hands when hauling in a heavy fish.

Gloves should always be worn when bringing in a fish. I learned the hard way that a powerful dorado doesn't really care what happens to your hands when it suddenly decides to make one more bolt for freedom.

The old fellow on Molokai impressed me with the method he used to rig the shock-absorbing tubing at the boat end of the trolling line.

He passed the line through a 30-inch length of 1/2" inside diameter surgical tubing, and tied a tightly cinched clove hitch around the end of the tubing with the trolling line itself. He then attached that end to a cleat in *Swan*'s cockpit and stretched the tubing as I held the line taut. When it was stretched near the extreme, he clamped the tubing tightly to

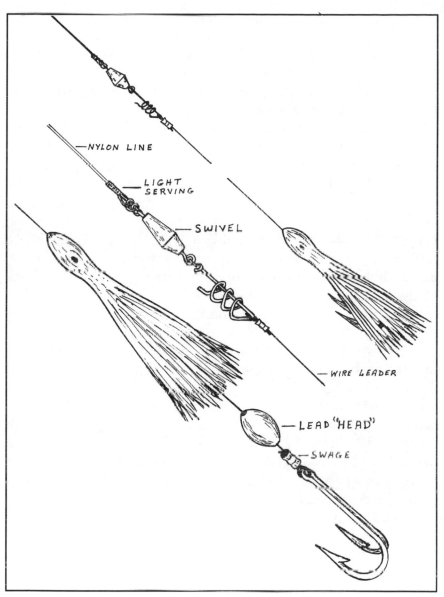

FIG. 11   *Rubber squid trolling lure*

the cord with his gnarled fist and let the tubing contract. The line coiled inside it like a spring.

"You catch 'em betta this rig," he said as he tied a clove hitch around the tubing where he had been gripping it.

It was neatly done! If the rubber broke, the line was still in

191

one piece. I whipped the clove hitches with waxed serving twine to prevent them from loosening.

The solution to the problem of knowing when a fish had hit was solved with a plastic clothespin. It required some shopping around to find a type that had a sufficiently strong spring.

A light line was passed through the center of the clothespin's spring and tied to one end of the surgical tubing. The ends of the tubing were brought together, forming a loop. The clothespin's jaws were clamped to a small eye tied in the trolling line where it left the tubing (See Fig. 12). When a fish hit, the line was jerked from the jaws of the pin with a sharp snap that was easily heard anywhere on board when sailing, and audible in the cockpit when motoring. Much of the shock of the strike was absorbed by the surgical tubing and the elasticity of the nylon line, lessening the chance of the hook being ripped from the mouth of the fish.

I constructed a simple device for winding in or streaming out the trolling line from small pieces of teak and hardwood doweling (See Fig. 13).

Occasionally the wire leader, hooks, and lures had to be replaced. A rubber squid can fare rather badly doing combat with a barracuda. These maintenance costs were minimal. With the exception of a crossing of the desolate South Atlantic, I cannot remember a passage in which we didn't catch at least one fish using the described gear.

Good fishing!

Sixty miles west of Jamaica, five days out of Portobelo, *Swan* reached north-by-west on the starboard tack. Everything was perfect! The last of the reefs and shoals lay well astern. *Swan*'s bow cut through white-crested waves of an ocean that was three miles deep. She was on course, sailing with a fair wind. In the Middle East, United States military forces and their allies were steamrolling across the desert. As if all of this were not enough, the wonderful aroma of Malaysian curry was wafting up from the galley—I was in Hog Heaven!

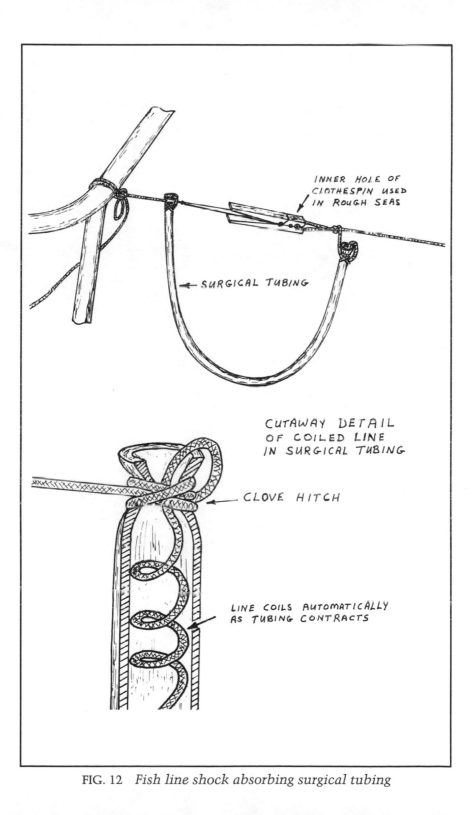

INNER HOLE OF
CLOTHESPIN USED
IN ROUGH SEAS

← SURGICAL TUBING

CUTAWAY DETAIL
OF COILED LINE
IN SURGICAL TUBING

CLOVE HITCH

LINE COILS AUTOMATICALLY
AS TUBING CONTRACTS

FIG. 12   *Fish line shock absorbing surgical tubing*

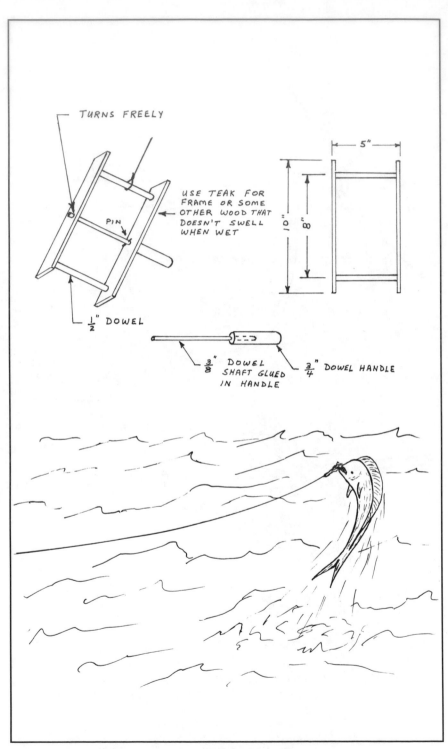

TURNS FREELY

USE TEAK FOR
FRAME OR SOME
OTHER WOOD THAT
DOESN'T SWELL
WHEN WET

PIN

5"

10"

8"

$\frac{1}{2}$" DOWEL

$\frac{3}{8}$" DOWEL
SHAFT GLUED
IN HANDLE

$\frac{3}{4}$" DOWEL HANDLE

FIG. 13 *Fish line winder*

Our landfall at Grand Cayman ranks as one of the most relaxed, executed-as-planned arrivals in our cruising experience.

As there wasn't a chance of making a daylight arrival on the following day at Georgetown, the port of entry at the western tip of Grand Cayman, we sailed a course to intersect a point 10 miles east and to windward of the island. From there we could run leisurely and safely along the leeward side of the well-lighted island during the night.

At 1830 on the following evening, a round of star sights and a bearing taken on a navigation light at the eastern end of the island fixed our position near the waypoint. We hove to and ate dinner with the lights of Georgetown illuminating the night sky.

With the aid of periodic bearings taken on the powerful navigation lights, Vane steered us downwind in the following seas at two knots under bare poles, three miles outside the island's leeward reefs. At 0400, near the western end of the island, we hove up beam to the wind and lay off until dawn.

There is a shallow, reef-lined lagoon at the southwestern tip of the island, and in it, lying at anchor, was *Patience*. What a surprise! We weren't sure where our friends had gone, with all of the variables that can influence a yacht's passage north from Panama.

This lagoon held another surprise in store that I will never forget. It nearly drowned me.

Georgetown had made a giant leap into the tourism world since we had last visited the island in 1980. Three cruise ships were lying at anchor in front of the town with a constant stream of ferries running between them and the landing. The old city dock where *Swan* had once moored in near isolation was long gone. The town was a different place with the same name.

Between the tax-haven banking business and the booming tourist industry, unemployment was near zero. The Cayman Islanders had turned their three coral-ringed islands into a 102-square-mile money machine. It had lost a bit of its quaintness and charm in the process, but I suppose the islanders had grown lean on a meager diet of charming quaintness.

We didn't see any derelict boats overloaded with Cayman Islanders trying to get out of their country, and we didn't see them standing around with their hands out. Conversely, we saw cruise ships and a procession of airliners bringing people into the island from all over the world with wallets full of money. Three flat little specks of sand and coral surrounded by pale-turquoise water making a grand go of it. We were impressed!

The clearing-in procedure included a visit by three members of the "Drug Squad." They were Keystone Cops on a mission, except they weren't really sure what it was. Apparently, they or someone in their department had found illegal drugs hidden in a yacht's freshwater tank. It appeared that they had concluded from this drug bust that this method of concealment of contraband was the modus operandi of *all* drug runners—period!

The three of them made a beeline to *Swan*'s forward water tank after I told them where it was located. They practically bumped their heads together trying to peer into the tank through the access port with flashlights.

When no cache of "stuff" was found in the tank, they looked in the oven. When that too failed to produce any incriminating evidence, they pronounced *Swan* immaculate and left. You couldn't put anything over on those boys!

We anchored near *Patience* in Southwest Bay. The bottom was almost solid coral with a few crevices where an anchor could get a tenuous bite. I never felt at ease with the situation, even after I dove and physically set the anchor.

We consumed a complete evening, a jug of wine, and a batch of Martha's conch fritters while we rehashed our runs through the Caribbean. As windward passages go, both had been good ones.

Two days later *Patience* sailed for Florida. It would have been a good thing for me if *Swan* had sailed on that day also; for that afternoon, spent in that sparkling coral lagoon, was very nearly the last one I would experience as a living, breathing human being.

Molly and I had spent that morning diving on the reef. We

found several well-developed conch to add to her shell collection. After lunch I rowed over to the reef to dive in search of the granddaddy of them all; a conch shell that would adorn our fireplace mantel one day.

Diving alone was a violation of the rules. We had allowed ourselves to grow careless about that during our long stay in the Sea of Cortez.

Near the reef I shipped the oars and lay over the transom, wearing a diving mask and snorkel. Beneath me, in perfect visibility, the coral formations glided past as the dinghy drifted with the current. The current was created by water that surged over the barrier reef, then emptied through a pass at the leeward end of the lagoon. A short distance from the pass, in an area of slightly deeper water than the rest of the lagoon, I dropped the anchor and slipped over the side.

For some time, perhaps three quarters of an hour, I swam on the surface against the current, diving often to examine a conch and set a choice one in a conspicuous spot to pick up on my return trip to the dinghy. Small fish, wary but curious, peered at me from the safety of niches in the reef.

Then, all of a sudden—in an instant—my store of energy was exhausted. Diving had so preoccupied me that I had not perceived my reserve of energy ebbing away. The last of it simply vanished. The constant exertion of swimming against the current and the repeated dives had sapped my strength to nearly zero.

My buoyancy appeared to have diminished with my strength. A sense of great danger descended upon me. In my frightened state I was attempting to keep my head above the choppy surface, which was difficult if not impossible in my exhausted condition.

In a twinkling, a carefree afternoon exploring a tropical reef had become a life-threatening situation.

A net bag that was fastened around my waist with a slippery hitch felt like tentacles entwined around my legs, intent on dragging me down. Panic welled up in me. I jerked the line at the hitch and the bag drifted away.

As I was gasping for air without the snorkel in my mouth,

a small wave hit me full in the face. Strangling on salt water, I ripped my face mask off and it sank. A frantic look at the dinghy told me that I had been swimming obliquely across the current. The dinghy was *not* downstream from me!

Pure, undiluted panic seized me; panic that exceeded anything I had ever experienced. My heart reacted to what must have been a massive jolt of adrenaline. It began to race, then pound violently. My vision became blurry—everything began swimming dizzily away in an aura of reddish light. I was fainting.

Soundlessly I screamed to myself: "Don't faint! Don't faint! You'll die if you faint!"

Miraculously, it worked. My head slowly cleared. Then I did what I should have done immediately. I turned on my back and floated—easily!

News of this wonderful turn of events took some time to reach my heart. It continued to beat like a runaway trip-hammer. Why it didn't self-destruct was a wonderment.

From the corner of my eye I saw the dinghy bobbing on the wavelets. Should I tax my overworked heart by swimming? It wasn't as if I had a choice! Besides, if my heart had survived the last few minutes it must be in pretty good shape.

I began swimming tentatively on my back with that awful but wonderful thumping sound still beating in my ears.

When I was about 10 yards from the dinghy I saw that I would miss it at the leisurely pace I was swimming. I turned over and swam flat-out across the current, just catching hold of the transom.

Cygnet, our baby swan that I had berated so many times for bumping the boat in the night or some such trivial thing was now cast in a different light.

After a few minutes of rest I hauled myself aboard and lay across the seats on my back. Overhead, scattered white clouds scudded across a pale-blue sky. It was a beautiful sight, taken for granted as so many things are; a beautiful sight that I viewed through tear-filled eyes.

For a long time I lay there thinking about that terrifying experience. That was as close as I had ever come to a date with the Grim Reaper, with the possible exception of when the double-drum sander went into orbit. I had lived a full life, but I wasn't quite ready for the final curtain.

I took in the anchor and started to row toward *Swan*, then I paused and looked back toward the reef. A sinking feeling came over me. The sight of it was chilling—menacing.

As I sat there, rowing in place, I knew I'd better deal with the thing right then. One bad moment out of hundreds of pleasant hours—it could turn into a bugaboo. Swimming and diving played too much of a part in our lives to let this experience cast a pall on it.

I turned and rowed back to the area where I had thrown off my mask. It was down there, bright orange, lying on the coral. I set the dinghy anchor, took more deep breaths than I needed, and dove down and retrieved the mask. With my courage bolstered, I made one more dive to gather up three conch that I had stacked near a coral head, then I rowed back to *Swan*.

"Well, did you have any luck?" Molly asked as I came alongside. I didn't know where to begin.

15

HITCHHIKING IS AN EASY WAY to travel around Grand Cayman Island. The price is right and it's pretty hard to get lost. A middle-aged lady, driving alone, made a U-turn and gave us a three-mile ride in the opposite direction of her destination. Grand Cayman is a long way from New York.

During our week-long stay on the island, it seemed that if we weren't walking or hitchhiking, we were preparing conch for the freezer. One does not eat a piece of conch like filet mignon. A rabid bulldog would be hard pressed to chew up the "foot" of a large conch. I was all for eating the small tender part and chucking the rest, like Bill Cody eating buffalo tongues, but Molly wouldn't hear of it.

We had both spent our early adolescence believing that we should eat our spinach, or whatever, because the children in China and other remote places were starving. It wasn't until I reached age seven or eight that I began to question the veracity of the logic which, in essence, held that if all the children in the United States went on a spinach-eating binge, it would create fat kids in China.

It was just possible that trace elements of the *original* China Syndrome subconsciously influenced Molly's feelings about not wasting food. Whatever the cause, her straightforward "waste not, want not" credo carried over to the bounty of the sea: We catch the food—we eat the food.

A hand-cranked food grinder made processing the conch an easy matter. It was a gift from Molly's mother, and it proved to be very useful during our voyages. Every blue-water cruiser should have one on board. These heavy, cast-iron grinders are not easy to find in a world of electrically operated food-processing gadgets. You may have to mow your Aunt Gertrude's lawn a few times to get her to turn loose that old-fashioned, reliable piece of equipment, and it will be well worth the effort.

In Mexico we used the grinder regularly to turn beef into hamburger. Cattle that managed to survive by grazing in the dry, barren hills surrounding Bahía de Los Angeles were a nutritionist's dream. They were totally fat-free and fibrous, like big hunks of lean beef jerky that walked. When one of the sinewy critters was slaughtered, the meat was "aged" for the time it took to carry it from the butchering shed to the little store where it was sold. A decent hamburger could be made from it after it was run through the grinder and reconstituted with a mixture of olive oil and water.

It was decision time. Our itinerary was open. We had charts for the Tennessee-Tombigbee Waterway and for most of the navigable rivers in the Central United States. We leaned toward the idea of a lazy drift through the inland river system. It was very appealing, but *Swan*'s six-foot draft posed a problem; it would seriously limit our mobility. A shoal-draft houseboat was much better suited for what we had in mind. We concluded that the river trip could be taken at a later period in our lives when we had given up adventuring on the high seas.

Our alternate plan was to meander north along the east coast of the United States via the Intracoastal Waterway. If the waterway became too confining, the Atlantic Ocean was just a right turn away.

The alternate plan was it. Our destination was Fort Myers on the west coast of Florida, which is located near the entrance to the waterway which cuts across the state and through Lake Okeechobee.

Our last night at Grand Cayman was spent anchored off the town, bathed in the brilliant light of two visiting cruise ships. In the morning, after we obtained our port clearance, we took one last swim in the incredibly clear water.

Viewed from beneath the surface, *Swan* appeared to be floating in air. Rising and falling in the gentle swell, she looked eager to get on with the voyage. Molly and I and our taut little ship had been through a lot, and it had nearly ended here, at least for me. During the two previous nights I had awakened drenched with perspiration from nightmares about a vortex of red light and my near-joining the ranks of the Dearly Departed. The dreams had been so vivid that my heart had convinced itself that The End was indeed near, and shifted into high gear. It had beaten faithfully some two billion times during my 55 years on the planet, and I had rewarded it for this tireless effort by jumping into the water and nearly scaring it to death. Of course, the aortic little fella doesn't go alone. Men my age were dropping like flies just mowing their lawns!

I had lain there, wondering if my heart was now in the category that I reserved for other nebulous things that I wondered about, like proof-coil anchor chain. Had my heart, like the weakest link in the chain, been so thoroughly and rigorously tested that it was fatigued and might burst at the drop of a hat? Finally, I had fallen asleep with a fuzzy vision of myself on the foredeck cranking the anchor windlass, neurotically wondering which would go first, my heart or the chain.

I drew a red line on the chart roughly parallel and 20 miles off the southern coast of Cuba. Inside the line I printed the words: Fidel Water.

With the reacher poled to port, *Swan* filled away from the island with a strong trade on the starboard quarter.

At the end of two days of effortless sailing we rounded Cabo San Antonio at the western tip of Cuba in the Yucatan Channel. The road got rougher when we sailed out of the protection of the land. Flying the close-hauled working jib and reefed main, *Swan* beat northward.

On day six we had managed to make enough easting to cross onto the huge bank that extends fully 135 miles into the Gulf of Mexico. The ride got rougher still.

Log entry February 4, 1991: Strong trades—headed—shallow—crashing & bashing.

As we neared the land the wind diminished and the seas lost their meanness. Sarasota was dead ahead. If the wind held we could fetch it close-hauled on the starboard tack before nightfall. It was 60 miles north of our destination, but suddenly it looked very inviting.

"Have you ever seen Sarasota in the early spring?" I called to Molly, as if I'd been there. "You'll love it!"

At 1500 we cranked up the engine to guarantee our daylight arrival. By 1800 we had cleared into the country by telephone and *Swan* was getting a well-deserved freshwater bath in a pricey $30 per night transient berth.

Fifty thousand miles had passed beneath *Swan*'s keel. She was purely a blue-water cruiser and did not take well to the confining waterway. After a brisk and carefree sail across Lake Okeechobee, she sneaked under a railroad bridge with only inches to spare and promptly ran aground. She wasn't used to scraping through tight spots. And she wasn't pleased about trading her dolphin friends for a bunch of surly alligators who peered at her through the reeds along the shore like submerged logs with eyes. But it was probably the manatees that finally drove *Swan* back out to sea. Not so much the manatees themselves, but the frequent warning signs that constrained her by law to avoid them like the plague. The problem was, no one on board, not even Vane, knew exactly what a manatee was. Finally, I shed some light on the problem by reading aloud the dictionary's definition of a manatee: "a tropical aquatic herbivorous mammal related to the dugong."

Related to the dugong! That was the final straw. At the next available pass to the Atlantic Ocean, a few miles north of Cape Canaveral, *Swan* returned to her natural element.

Marine weather reports were favorable for the 400-mile passage to Beaufort, North Carolina, across the bight formed by the Georgia and South Carolina coastline. I plotted a sailing track that would intercept the north-setting Gulf Stream and clear Frying Pan Shoals off Cape Fear.

In 20 knots of chilly wind, *Swan* close-reached briskly off the land. To protect the cockpit from the wind and the occasional blast of spray that flew over the weathercloths, I rigged a canvas windbreak from the forward part of the dodger to the windward backstay. With this fortification against the elements in place, First Mate Hypothermia ventured out of the cabin to enjoy the warmth of the sun.

In line with the weather forecast, the wind moved in a clockwise direction and remained a steady Force 5. Sailing in the heart of the current, *Swan* chalked up a 158-mile day flying only the reacher in a quartering wind that had warmed considerably.

Skirting Frying Pan Shoals, *Swan* ran before the wind into Onslow Bay in the approaches to Beaufort. Although local fishing boats were cutting the Beaufort Inlet channel buoys very close to land, it was an unfamiliar port to us. We went by the book and entered the ship channel at the outer marker.

The historic, seafaring town of Beaufort was a place where we could see ourselves spending some time. We needed a temporary address where we could receive our stacked-up mail, and it would be a good place to leave *Swan* while we visited our relatives.

The town had a delightful ambience; it was, at once, kinetic and laid back. Beaufort was a "must" stop for yachts migrating north and south in the waterway as the seasons dictated.

Many of Beaufort's stately homes, some with widow's walks atop them, were built in the early 19th century. They were unscathed by the Civil War, but as the cemetery in the heart of town attests, this was not the case for many of the town's inhabitants.

On that first evening in Beaufort, the strains of guitars and singing drifted across the anchorage from a waterfront bandstand. The singer was doing a fair imitation of Jimmy Buffett: ". . . wasting away again in Margaritaville—searching for my lost shaker of salt . . ." The song caused us to wonder where all the boats were that spent that memorable season with us in the Sea of Cortez—the good times at Bahía de Los Angeles; Don Juan; Concepción.

Now the singer was "changing latitudes—changing attitudes." We had changed our latitude some, and our longitude a lot; but our attitudes about following our dreams hadn't changed at all, from what I could tell. I wondered if they ever would.

Epilogue

THE DOORBELL RANG at my uncle and aunt's home in Florida where we were visiting. I opened the door. "Package for Jim Moore," a United Parcel Service delivery man said in a properly urgent manner.

I stood in the kitchen holding the package. It was from the book publisher. I was about to see the fruits of a long writing effort. A montage of thoughts passed quickly through my mind: Molly endlessly typing—wadded balls of discarded writing paper in *Swan*'s cockpit—my trip through the Mexican desert to California to complete the book contract business—the cucumber man.

Suddenly, my reverie was interrupted by Molly's excited voice behind me. "Open it! Open it! It's the book!" As if maybe I thought it was a bundle of dirty laundry.

My immediate reaction was to tease her by opening the parcel slowly and deliberately, but she wouldn't stand for it. She grabbed the package from my hands. She was a kid out of control on Christmas morning, Rip! Rip! It was opened in a flash and she held up three copies of *By Way of the Wind*!

It was quite a moment—icing on the cake. For 18 years we had done almost exactly what we wanted to do, and now we had a book published about our adventures. The entire experience, from the germination of the idea to build a boat and sail it to the South Pacific, to holding a copy of our book in our hands, had exceeded our most optimistic hopes and dreams. It suddenly seemed a good time to take stock of our lives again.

We had spent 14 of the past 18 years living and cruising aboard *Swan*; and our marriage, which could hardly be considered normal in the sense of a home in the suburbs and nine-to-five jobs, was none the worse for it. I should emphasize that this favorable assessment of our married life was purely subjective, as we weren't really sure what a marriage was supposed to be like after 14 years on a 36-foot sailboat.

(All Indians walk in single file—at least the only one I ever knew did.) People with cruising plans have frequently asked Molly and me our opinion of how marriages fare in the cruising lifestyle. Generally, we feel that a marriage that falls apart while the couple is living and cruising aboard a boat would most likely fail on the land also. It would just take a little longer.

Another question often asked by these would-be voyagers concerns the cost of cruising and how we handled money transfers. Before leaving Oregon on our first voyage we obtained a list of banks in foreign countries that were correspondent banks with our Portland bank. Our savings account was flagged with a note stating that requests for fund transfers to foreign banks would be received from us from time to time.

Twice during the circumnavigation we had money transferred; once in New Zealand and later in South Africa. Upon arriving in those countries we opened a savings account to receive the fund transfers. We then wrote a letter to our Portland bank requesting the money. Molly and I both signed the letter to give the bank an additional signature as verification of the authenticity of the transfer request, although only one signature was actually required. Setting it up for either one of our signatures was important, because funds could still be obtained in the event that one of us was incapacitated.

The transaction required about one week to complete. With the use of facsimile machines, it may now take only hours.

Most of our cruising funds were carried in the form of traveler's checks. They were kept in a strongbox that I had built into a locker with the locking nuts of the mounting bolts inside the box, thus making them inaccessible unless the box was opened. It also held our passports and other important papers.

The locker containing the strongbox was completely emptied during the burglarizing of *Swan* in Costa Rica, but the contents of the box were untouched. Any security measure can be circumvented; however, a strongbox at least thwarts the larcenous plans of an unprepared sneak thief.

As a precaution against finding ourselves flat broke in some remote spot as a result of theft or a logistical miscalculation, I built a small hidden compartment in *Swan* large enough to hold ten $100 dollar bills and a copy of the boat's title. We could have easily sailed to the United States from anywhere in the world with $1000, and if a dispute concerning the rightful ownership of *Swan* somehow developed, producing the title from the hidden compartment in the presence of law officers would be very useful in settling the matter.

With all of the variables involved, estimating the cost of cruising is a guesstimate at best, and I wouldn't consider attempting it. However, I know the approximate amount of money that we spent, and this information might be useful in the preparation of one's cruising budget.

Adjusted for inflation to 1993 dollars, we spent a rough average of $6300 per year during all of our cruising years. This covered all *routine* boat maintenance, our normal living expenses, and incidental expenses such as an occasional car rental. It did not include the costs of "repowering" while we were in California, or the refit in Honolulu.

We had no fixed costs such as boat payments. *Swan's* title was free and clear the day Molly christened her with a bottle of champagne, and we carried boat insurance only while sailing in American waters because of the exorbitant cost of carrying no-territorial-limit insurance.

As I am a jack-of-all-trades (yes, I know the next line), I was able to do almost all of the maintenance on *Swan* with the assistance of my able mate. This helped keep our cruising costs down, of course, and it actually allowed us to live better than our annual budget suggests. Also, *Swan* was built so solidly that she didn't nickel-and-dime the cruising kitty at every turn.

I believe that the truly free cruiser is the person who has distilled his situation down to a well-found boat and a bank account. We have seen cruisers who spent a good portion of their time trying to manage their properties and complex financial affairs by radio, telephone, carrier pigeon, or whatever. If you cannot reasonably divest yourself of the responsibility of business or property, or don't care to do so, my advice would be to hire a professional to handle the day-to-day problems that will inevitably arise. I would be leery about counting on Uncle Joe to handle your affairs for you as he said he would when he was in an expansive mood at the Christmas party.

On both of our voyages we were in the "truly free" category. We wouldn't have had it any other way.

And now, once again, we were at a cruising crossroads. We talked randomly about our options as we strolled along the Beaufort waterfront, followed by a large yellow dog that Molly had "borrowed." We both loved dogs, but felt that they presented too many problems on a cruising boat, so Molly borrowed dogs at every opportunity when we were in port.

"We could sail over to the Mediterranean and do that Columbus thing," Molly said in a matter-of-fact way, as if crossing the Atlantic Ocean was just another Sunday afternoon sail. It was hard to believe that this was the same person speaking, who, in 1973, had had a habit of referring to the bow of the newly arrived hull of the future *Swan* as "the pointed end." She then said, "Or maybe we should get a dog."

We sat down on the edge of the dock in the warmth of the late afternoon sun with Rent-a-Dog between us. I repeated Molly's words slowly to myself: "We could do that . . . Columbus thing. Or maybe we should get . . . a dog."

BEAUFORT SCALE OF WIND

BEAUFORT NUMBER	DESCRIPTIVE TERM	SPECIFICATIONS	WIND SPEED IN KNOTS
0	Calm	Sea like a mirror	1
1	Light air	Ripples with the appearance of scales are formed, but without foam crests	1–3
2	Light breeze	Small wavelets; still short but more pronounced crests have a glassy appearance and do not break	4–6
3	Gentle breeze	Large wavelets; crests begin to break; foam of glassy appearance; perhaps scattered white horses	7–10
4	Moderate breeze	Small waves, becoming longer; fairly frequent white horses	11–16
5	Fresh breeze	Moderate waves, taking a more pronounced long form; many white horses are formed (chance of some spray)	17–21
6	Strong breeze	Large waves begin to form; the white foam crests are more extensive everywhere (probably some spray)	22–27
7	Near gale	Sea heaps up and white foam from breaking waves begins to be blown in streaks along the direction of the wind	28–33
8	Gale	Moderately high waves of greater length; edges of crests begin to break into the spindrift; the foam is blown in well-marked streaks along the direction of the wind	34–40

BEAUFORT NUMBER	DESCRIPTIVE TERM	SPECIFICATIONS	WIND SPEED IN KNOTS
9	Strong gale	High waves; dense streaks of foam along the direction of the wind; crests of waves begin to topple, tumble and roll over; spray affects visibility	41–47
10	Storm	Very high waves with long overhanging crests; the resulting foam, in great patches, is blown in dense white streaks along the direction of the wind; on the whole, the surface of the sea takes a white appearance; the tumbling of the sea becomes heavy and shock-like; visibility affected	48–55
11	Violent storm	Exceptionally high waves (small and medium-sized ships might be for a time lost to view behind the waves); the sea is completely covered with long white patches of foam lying along the direction of the wind; everywhere the edges of the wave crests are blown into froth, visibility affected	56–63
12	Hurricane	The air is filled with foam and spray; sea completely white with driving spray; visibility very seriously affected	64 and over

THE FIRST VOYAGE OF *SWAN*

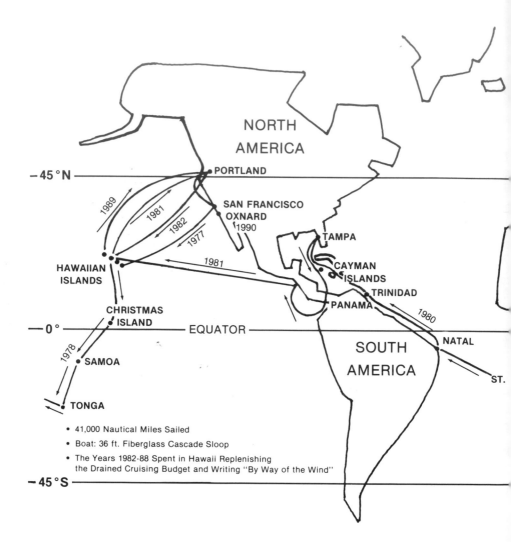

NORTH AMERICA

−45°N — PORTLAND

1989

1981

1982

1977

SAN FRANCISCO
OXNARD
1990

TAMPA

1981

HAWAIIAN
ISLANDS

CAYMAN
ISLANDS

TRINIDAD

CHRISTMAS
ISLAND

PANAMA

−0° — EQUATOR —

SOUTH
AMERICA

1980

NATAL

1978

SAMOA

ST.

TONGA

- 41,000 Nautical Miles Sailed
- Boat: 36 ft. Fiberglass Cascade Sloop
- The Years 1982-88 Spent in Hawaii Replenishing
  the Drained Cruising Budget and Writing "By Way of the Wind"

−45°S